E. F. Richards

My mother's cook Book

E. F. Richards

My mother's cook Book

ISBN/EAN: 9783744789707

Printed in Europe, USA, Canada, Australia, Japan

Cover: Foto ©Andreas Hilbeck / pixelio.de

More available books at **www.hansebooks.com**

MY MOTHER'S

COOK BOOK

COMPILED BY

LADIES OF ST. LOUIS,

AND SOLD FOR THE BENEFIT OF THE

WOMEN'S CHRISTIAN HOME.

> "Cookery is an Art,
> Still changing and of momentary triumph.
> Know, on thyself thy genius must depend;
> All books of Cookery, all helps of Art,
> Are vain, if void of genius thou wouldst cook."

SAINT LOUIS:
HUGH R. HILDRETH PRINTING COMPANY, 407 N. FOURTH STREET.
1880.

MY MOTHER'S COOK BOOK.

WHAT an euphonious title!—one we would not venture to change or presume to rival in many respects; but as we (the daughters) are living in an age of progress, we will venture to suggest, without any disrespect to our mothers, that while their theories were perfect, we wish to add some suggestions and recipes, which, in our experience, we have found successful, and great improvements on the former editions, and have won for us from "the lords of creation" the pleasing commendation, "Wife, your cooking of this (or that) dish has outdone our mothers—a thing we considered impossible."

In view of these most wonderful achievements in household good, we have been stimulated to add new recipes, and to send this Cook Book forth into the world, confident of success, as every young housekeeper who is encountering the "fiery trials of life," will find remedies for most of the ills that flesh is heir to, and the means of securing happiness, and sunshine too, for her household, following Solomon's advice, "giving meat to her household and a portion to her maidens," WELL COOKED and palatable.

CONTRIBUTORS.

Mrs. T. J. ALBRIGHT, Kirkwood.
" CORNELIA BEER, St. Louis.
Prof. BLOT.
Mrs. CHAS. CULLIS, Boston.
" SAM'L COPP, St. Louis.
" J. G. CHAPMAM, St. Louis.
" S. C. CUMMINS, St. Louis.
" HUGH CAMPBELL.
" WM. CLAFLIN, Boston.
" J. T. DAVIS, St. Louis.
" H. N. DAVIS, St. Louis.
" ADMIRAL DUPONT.
" WM. G. ELIOT, St. Louis.
" T. B. EDGAR, St. Louis.
" EZRA FARNSWORTH, Boston.
" R. F. FROST, Boston.
" HENRY FARNUM, Boston.
" O. D. FILLEY, St. Louis.
" GILES F. FILLEY, St. Louis.
" U. S. GRANT.
" S. T. GLOVER, St. Louis.
Miss E. L. GLOVER, St. Louis.

Mrs. A. M. GARDNER, St. Louis.
" H. HENDERSON, Maryland.
" LEWIS E. KLINE, St. Louis.
" J. M. KRUM, St. Louis.
" S. LARKIN, St. Louis.
" J. B. LOUDERMAN, St. Louis.
" GEO. LEIGHTON, St. Louis.
" H. McKITTRICK, St. Louis.
" R. H. MORTON, St. Louis.
" H. C. MOORE, St. Louis.
" WM. NOYES, St. Louis.
" N. W. PERKINS, St. Louis.
" D. R. POWELL, St. Louis.
" AVERY PLUMMER, Boston.
" T. T. RICHARDS, St. Louis.
" E. F. RICHARDS, St. Louis.
" S. A. RANLETT, St. Louis.
" JOSEPH STORY, Boston.
" SAM'L TREAT, St. Louis.
" LOUISE VOGT, St. Louis.
" SHEPARD WELLS, St. Louis.
" D. C. YOUNG, St. Louis.
OTHERS.

PREFACE.

A GENUINE Cook Book. Not a series of experimental conjectures evolved from the consciousness of a brilliant theorist in cooking, but a batch of practical recipes that have been embodied in luscious dishes, and bear the credentials of gratified appetites.

This is an attempt to falsify that sad proverb: "The Lord sends food—cooks come from *another direction.*" This book proves that food and cooks may *both* have a celestial origin. This is the domestic balm in Gilead. Here may the gratified husband find all those marvellous puddings, pies and pickles with which "his mother" stimulated and appeased his appetite when he was a clothes-consuming, cotton-headed school-boy. Here may the youth who is shedding his primal petticoats find the miraculous viands with which grandma has made Saturday afternoon a foretaste of Heaven. Here may the timid, trembling, untried housekeeper, transplanted from her home of luxury to the three-roomed "straight jimmie" of a struggling and poverty-burdened husband, find herself transformed into a $4,000 French cook; while the world-wearied, exacting husband, who has worked into the tapestry that adorns the walls of his poor wife's memory the dreary words: "You ought to have seen how MY MOTHER could make it;" or filled her brain with the raven-like monotone: "Mother knew *how* to cook," will find "my mother's" brilliant successes reproduced, and will be forced to acknowledge that if Paradise was lost by an apple, it may be regained by an apple pie.

This book will render Divorce Courts an expensive luxury, instead of a social necessity. It is the housekeeper's Magna Charta. Her Emancipation Proclamation. It is the first eloquent muttering of the domestic revolution by which Ethiopia and Hibernia will be hurled from their throne, the Saxon race regain its supremacy, and those terrible kitchen mandates issued by Bridget and Dinah, before which the young wife was wont to tremble and turn pale, will be as powerless as the Pope's bull against the comet.

The recipes gathered into this priceless volume have been sent from all parts of the known world; several even from New Jersey. Many delicacies were expected from the centre of Africa, by the courtesy of Stanley, but these have been unavoidably detained. King "Calico," remembering gratefully the hospitality of the "Future Great," has sent a rare and valuable recipe of his grandfather's, of a delicious preparation of cold missionary and queen olives, while an amiable and almond-eyed celestial sends a recipe for the cooking of a common and inexpensive domestic rodent. But these delicacies are withheld out of deference to venerable prejudices.

Yet the most fastidious alderman need not dread famine. Here is a wilderness of pies, puddings, pickles, jellies and jams; here are more cookies and cream pies than could be found at a charitable Sunday-school picnic; every species of pie, except the "humble pie" of Uriah Heep; mince pies so concentrated in power, that a cubic inch is guaranteed to produce a kaleidoscopic vision of your grandmother; pickles of such potency that they are warranted to produce that delicate greenness of complexion and angularity of contour so much prized by young damsels in their earliest *gigglehood*, and popularly supposed to be solely the fruit of a free consumption of slate pencils.

The book reaches its eloquent culmination in the production of a *Hash*, in whose complex composition may be found representatives from the entire animal and vegetable kingdoms. As the secret of its structure has been hidden from the foundation of the world, it is appropriately called "mystery." This recipe alone is worth the price of the book. It is the triumph of eclecticism. It simplifies social economy by absolutely preventing waste. It is the redemption of the Boarding House. It will ultimately promote the interests of general education by transforming the college hash from what it is into "a thing of beauty and a joy forever."

MEASURE.

Wheat Flour..1 pound is 1 quart.
Indian Meal...1 pound 2 ounces is 1 quart.
Butter, when soft..1 pound is 1 quart.
Loaf Sugar, broken..1 pound is 1 quart
White Sugar, powdered...1 pound 1 ounce is 1 quart.
Best Brown Sugar...1 pound 2 ounces is 1 quart.
Ten Eggs..are 1 quart.
Flour..four pecks are 1 bushel.
16 large teaspoonfuls...are 1 pint.
8   "   "   ....are 1 gill.
4   "   "   ....are ½ gill.
A common size tumbler...is ½ pint.
    "   "   wine glass...is ½ gill.
A tea cup..is 1 gill.
A large wine glass ....is 1 gill.
A large tablespoonful...is ½ ounce.
40 drops equal to..1 teaspoonful.
4 teaspoonfuls equal to...1 tablespoonful.

A WORD ABOUT COOKING.

Assuming that the recipes contained in this book, for the preparation of our food, have been compiled with all the care that skill and experience could suggest, we are naturally led a step further, to inquire whether these beneficent results are not too frequently neutralized in those succeeding stages which attend the cooking of the food itself. While we cannot overestimate the importance of good wholesome cooking to the health and comfort of our daily life, there is no department in which its fundamental rules are less understood or more generally disregarded.

Count Rumford, who spent a life-time in experimenting upon the best modes of cooking, has given to the world the true theory, which has been confirmed by experience, and may be summed up in the sentence—

USE LESS FUEL, AND TAKE LONGER TIME.

He urges the economical use of heat by using but little fuel, and taking more time in all its various operations; for it is strictly true, that good cooking *cannot be done in a hurry*

For instance, a loaf of bread cannot be thoroughly baked in less than one hour. A sufficient time must be allowed for the generation of the gas produced by yeast, which gives the loaf when done its spongy character that renders it light and wholesome. To secure this result the oven must not be too hot. A temperature of 350 degrees is the utmost required for any kind of bread. The process is greatly aided, and a highly favorable result secured, by placing the equivalent of a saucer of water in the oven with the bread while baking.

It may be well at this point to suggest *how to regulate the Stove.*

When the oven is well heated, place within it the article to be baked, and at once *close the front draft* as far as possible, simply admitting just enough air to carry off the smoke, after which two sticks of wood (or their equivalent) are sufficient to complete the work.

For *roasting meats* a still less heat is required than for bread—a temperature of 200 degrees being enough, and better than more: but it is well to remember that the presence of water in the oven is as essential in the cooking of meats as in baking bread. A most excellent plan is adopted of using *two* drip pans, one within the other, the larger one containing the water, while the meat is placed in the smaller one.

Meats should always be *well basted* at intervals during the process of cooking.

An observance of these simple rules will effectually remove all complaints which follow the ignorant use of the modern oven, and we shall no more be reminded of the superiority of meats roasted before the fire "*as my mother used to do it.*"

At the risk of repeating what has already been said, we cannot too strongly urge that the true secret of baking either meats or bread consists in using BUT A SMALL QUANTITY OF FUEL.

As a rule, one-half the usual weight consumed is ample to do the work, and do it well; a saving is thus effected in

A WORD ABOUT COOKING.

the cost of fuel and in the wear and tear of the stove as well, while the work is done much more satisfactorily.

Whilst we advocate the use of a small quantity of fuel to do good cooking, we also recommend the use of large cooking stoves to do the work of a family. Large stoves are cheaper in proportion to their size than smaller ones. The plates are usually heavier, they will last longer, and as a rule do better cooking. The plates of a stove should *never* be made *red-hot;* whenever this is the case, it is certain that there is too much fuel used. Iron at red heat, visible by day, shows a temperature of over a thousand degrees; at red heat, visible in twilight, of over 800 degrees; bright red in the dark, of over seven hundred and fifty degrees; which is more than twice the amount of heat required for any ordinary cooking. Coal is more difficult to manage than wood; where it is used great care should be taken, using as small a quantity as possible. What has been said in regard to cooking stoves applies as well to heating stoves, for both economy and durability.

MY MOTHER'S COOK BOOK.

SOUPS.

The best soups are made from fresh bones and raw meat simmered gently for five or six hours. Soups ought never to boil fast, and every particle of grease must be carefully skimmed off. After cooking some time it is better to set aside until the next day, and then it ought to be a jelly, from which all the grease and sediment must be wiped off. The second day this stock can be put on about two hours before dinner, add the vegetables chopped or grated fine, salt, pepper, celery seed or tops, and about one-half tablespoonful of butter rubbed into two tablespoonfuls of flour for thickening. Have some toasted bread cut into small squares in the tureen and pour over the soup.

Soups can be made much richer by seasoning with any of the ketchups or meat sauces, such as Worcestershire sauce, walnut ketchup, etc.; summer savory, sweet marjoram and celery seeds are also nice; a glass of wine, eggs boiled hard and chopped fine, orange cut in very fine pieces, without peeling. Some like lemon, while to others it ruins the soup, so the best plan is to slice the lemons and pass around after the soup is served. To make soups dark thicken with flour that has been browned in the oven, or brown sugar burnt black; stale bread toasted in the oven rolled fine, makes a nice thickening. The general rule in making soup is to allow one pound of meat to one quart of water.

PEA SOUP.

A pint and a half of split peas; two small onions; pepper and salt to taste. Use three quarts of water and boil from five to six hours. Pork is often put in, but makes the soup far less wholesome. If the water is hard, add a piece of saleratus not larger than a pea. It would be difficult to find a way in which the same amount of nourishment could be obtained for four times what this cost.—HEARTH AND HOME.

BROWN SOUP.

Take a beef shin and boil all day until it will become a jelly, when cold, strain it and set away until the next day. Then take a piece of butter size of an egg, a large onion; brown together in the same pan, then put in two or three tablespoonfuls of brown flour, two carrots if small, two turnips if small, piece of celery, little thyme, little parsley, allspice, mace, cloves, to taste. I generally take three or four cloves, one piece of mace (small), little pinch of allspice; if you have not Chili pepper use common pepper; salt, Worcestershire sauce. Let it cook slowly all day. When the vegetables are thoroughly cooked, press them well through the strainer to get all the substance; put in a little macaroni, heaping wine glass of sherry wine, force meat balls; let the macaroni cook, then serve it.

MRS. W. MAURICE.

CHICKEN GUMBO.

Disjoint an old chicken and fry brown in hot lard, afterwards fry in the same lard a small piece of ham, one-half the size of your hand, and a sliced onion; put it into the kettle with four quarts of boiling water, and boil slowly for four hours; one quart of sliced gumbo and one pint of sliced tomatoes (or a whole can if in winter); corn or celery tops improves it, one-half dozen cloves, pepper and salt to taste. Serve with boiled rice.

VEAL SOUP.

Put into a pot a knuckle of veal that has been cracked in three or four places and carefully washed to get off all the little pieces of bone; cover with about one gallon of water and let it simmer from two to three hours, the longer the better, skim well; about one hour and a half before dinner, add a little onion, pieces of minced celery or celery seed, salt, pepper; as veal makes a white soup it is very nice to add two cups of vermicelli or macaroni broken in inch pieces; or the same vegetables may be added and in the same way as for beef soup. Veal soup can be used the same day as made.

VEAL SOUP.

Boil a knuckle of veal with a cup of rice; set it away till next day, add four eggs, one lemon, a little salt; strain it, beat the eggs and lemon together in the tureen, and pour the soup on it.   MRS. SAM'L TREAT.

BEEF SOUP.

Take a bone with a nice piece of meat attached to it, have the bone cracked in two or three places so as to get the marrow, then cover with three or four quarts of water; let it boil slowly for four hours or more, skimming well all the time, then put aside until the next day. About two hours before dinner skim off all the fat and grease which will be found caked on top of the soup, pour off carefully from the sediment at the bottom, then cook again, adding such vegetables as you may wish; tomatoes, gumbo, a red pepper, a soup bunch having the parsley minced fine, the carrot grated, the onion and other things chopped fine; season with salt, thicken with a little flour and butter rubbed together; before serving, some prefer to have all the pieces of meat and thick part of vegetables strained out.

BLACK BEAN SOUP.

Soak one quart of beans over night, and keep them warm; drain off the water; add fresh; cook gently four or five hours, adding water as it boils away; season with salt, pepper and cloves, while cooking. When done, strain thoroughly; put in three slices of lemon, a sliced hard-boiled egg, and small pieces of toasted bread. Stock can be used instead of water.

BEAN SOUP.

One soup-bone, four or five pounds; one soup-bunch; one pint of beans, soaked over night. Boil the meat in a gallon and a half of water, for two hours; skim when it comes to a boil. Put in the soup-bunch cut up; three or four sliced potatoes; three or four sliced onions, fried in a tablespoonful of lard; dredge in four tablespoonfuls of browned flour; season; if any more water is needed, add it boiling. Boil all for three hours. Strain before serving.

MARY COLBURT.

SOUR DOCK SOUP.

Take a quantity of the greens, clean the leaves from the stems. Put in a sauce-pan a piece of butter, when melted put in the greens, let it come to a stew. Pour in a cup or two of water; when boiled, take the yolks of two eggs, beat with three tablespoonfuls of cream; stir in and it is finished; add a little salt. This is an excellent dish for the sick.

LOUISE VOGT.

MOCK TURTLE SOUP.

First day. Take one large calf's head, with skin on; let the butcher open; remove the eyes and nose; wash in cold water several times. Take out the brains, skin and tie them in a thin cloth; put in a pot with the head and three quarts of water. Skim carefully, while boiling one hour; take out the brains and put aside; add to the soup two onions, two turnips, one leek, a bunch of parsley; cover and let stand where it boils gently seven hours. At the same time put in a second pot, one old hen, a knuckle of veal and three quarts water; boil seven hours; let stand over night and skim off the fat next morning. Second day. Take a stew pan that holds six quarts, put on the fire with one-half pound good butter, twelve ounces sliced onions, four ounces green sage; let this fry one hour, then add the entire contents of the two pots cooked the day previous, and season the whole with one-half ounce black pepper, one-fourth ounce ground allspice, one tablespoonful salt and one of curry powder, little cayenne pepper, the yellow rind of one lemon grated. Let all simmer gently two hours, stirring often to prevent meat sticking. Strain through a cotton bag into a clean pot, add one-half pint of Madeira wine, juice of one lemon, boil one hour, and add meat balls while boiling and just before the soup is done. To thicken, brown and rub smoothly one pound of flour into one-fourth pound of butter in a frying pan, add some of the soup by degrees until it is thin enough to pour into the soup; this must be added after straining and before boiling the last hour. Meat balls: Chop the brains already boiled with a pinch of dried thyme, the grated peel of one lemon, mix all with two eggs and flour to roll into balls size of a pigeon's egg, and fry in butter. Egg balls (if preferred): The yolk of one egg and flour roll in small balls; or use the yolks of twelve hard boiled eggs; place in the tureen and pour over the soup just before serving.

MOCK TURTLE SOUP.

One pound of butter; one-half pound of flour; two onions; two carrots; allspice, sage and thyme; whole pepper; nutmeg; slice of ham; one calf's head, boiled and cut small. Boil the head gradually for three or four hours, skimming the grease off; then add four quarts of stock, made of any kind of meat. Make egg balls of the yolks of hard boiled eggs, mixed with a little flour; also meat balls, made of veal cut very fine, mixed with the yolks of two raw eggs; add just before serving. Color with a spoonful of burnt brown sugar. Ten minutes before dishing, add half a glass of brandy and Madeira wine.

GUMBO SOUP.

Fry a knuckle of veal in butter, with pepper, salt and onions; after it is fried, add three dozen ochra, skinned, with the ends cut off, and a piece of ham. Pour two gallons of boiling water on this; when about half cooked, add four crabs; first boil them and divide each in four parts, frying them brown, with butter, pepper and salt. About two hours before dinner, add one dozen tomatoes, with the skins taken off.

GUMBO SOUP.

Fry five or six slices of salt-pork; after they are done, fry six large onions in the same fat; cut up and fry a good sized chicken; put these into a large pot with a small piece of lean ham and two quarts of water; when it boils put in one quart of sliced gumbo and the corn cut from two ears, a few tomatoes if you like, and a small piece of red pepper, no salt. Keep adding boiling water as it boils away. It should be on the fire five or six hours.

Miss Emily Tucker.

GUMBO SOUP.

Fry one large chicken or a knuckle of veal with two or three onions in a little lard until brown, put them in a soup kettle with a quart of gumbo sliced fine, and a quart of tomatoes previously peeled and sliced; add a gallon and a half of water, half a red pepper; boil slowly four or five hours and stir frequently with a wooden spoon.

Mrs. C. B. Richards.

MOCK OYSTER SOUP.

One pint tomatoes, well stewed; one quart boiling water; put in a teaspoonful of soda; when it has done foaming add one quart boiling milk; a piece of butter, size of an egg. Salt and pepper to taste. Pour upon three soda crackers rolled.

Mrs. Sam'l Copp.

PILAF—TURKISH DISH.

Prepare a rich beef soup; season with tomatoes, pepper and salt; and while it is boiling add about half the quantity of rice, well washed; let the two boil together twenty minutes, or until the soup is entirely absorbed by the rice. Melt quickly half a pound of best butter, mix immediately with the rice, and serve in five minutes. If desired to have meat in the Pilaf, take either chicken, turkey, or lamb, roasted, cut in small pieces, and put it in the rice while boiling, ten minutes before taking from the fire, and before putting on the butter. MRS. JASIGI.

TURTLE SOUP.

You must have the turtle alive; cut the head off and let it bleed to death. Boil the turtle till the shells can be separated, and the meat is cooked. Take off the gall bladder, and if you find a black ball (if there is any) throw it away. Put butter and flour in a sauce pan, and the pieces of turtle and cook a little; pour in some broth; put in your dish a lemon cut in slices, an egg boiled and cut up; pour over it the soup and meat and serve. PROF. BLOT.

BLACK, OR TURTLE BEAN SOUP.

Take two teacups of beans, and soak them in water over night; then add three quarts of stock; let it boil three hours; adding mace, cinnamon, allspice and pepper, according to taste; two onions; pass through the cullender, and then through the sieve; put in the tureen the juice of two lemons, four eggs boiled hard and chopped fine, a little Harvey sauce, then pour the soup on it.

MRS. CHAS. CULLIS, Boston.

TOMATO SOUP.

Twelve tomatoes, peeled and cooked, or one quart can; one tablespoonful soda; one quart milk; season with salt and pepper; just before taking up, put in half a pint of crackers or bread crumbs, piece of butter size of an egg.

TOMATO SOUP.

One quart sliced tomatoes; two quarts cold water; a little rice. Let it come to a boil; a pinch of soda; then add two cups of milk; two tablespoonfuls of butter; one tablespoonful of flour; salt and pepper to taste. Boil ten minutes.

Mrs. H. D. Hutch, Kirkwood.

TOMATO SOUP.

Take a nice beef bone (marrow is best); boil in one gallon of water four hours, adding hot water if necessary; then add one quart of tomatoes and two onions (medium size) chopped fine, and a few celery tops; boil one and a half hours, and serve. This soup is best the second day.

Mrs. Rainwater.

POTATO SOUP.

Boil together one dozen large potatoes and three onions, till soft; mash them through a cullender, and stir them into one quart of boiling milk. Season with butter, pepper and salt.

Mrs. F. G. Goddard.

LOBSTER SOUP.

Chop the lobster fine; add the green part; three crackers pounded fine; a good sized piece of butter; have one quart of milk just scalded and turn over it, then put all together and bring to a boil.

Mrs. Nath. Walker, Boston.

PHILADELPHIA PEPPER POT.

To four quarts of water put one pound corned pork and two pounds neck mutton or veal, cook slowly three hours, then take out the mutton; put into the broth four turnips, and if in season, six or eight tomatoes, one onion, a piece of red pepper, and a very little salt. Have ready boiled one-fourth pound of nice tripe cut into small pieces, put them in with six potatoes sliced thin, and one pint bowl of nice light dumplings dropped very small. Simmer altogether one hour.

CALF'S HEAD SOUP.

Cover the head well with water and boil until very tender. Cut the meat from the bones, keeping the brains. Have ready three large onions chopped fine, one nutmeg grated, one teaspoonful of ground cloves and two of cinnamon; put the meat and spices into the pot with a small cup of butter, pour the broth over and stew one hour; salt and pepper to taste. When ready to serve put in the brains, the juice of one lemon, one cup of claret and two spoonfuls of walnut catchup.   MISS EMILY TUCKER.

BEEF BOUILLI.

Take the face of the rump and put it on to boil about four hours; after it has been on half an hour skim it well, then add carrots and turnips cut up fine; roast one onion brown on the coals, stick it with cloves and put it in; add half a tumbler of red wine (port is better), a little tomato or other catchup, cayenne, or any other good thing. Before serving take out some of the gravy in a teacup and cut up a pickled cucumber into slices and pour over the beef.
      MRS. SAM'L TREAT.

BEEF BOUILLI.

Wash five or six pounds of the round of beef thoroughly in cold water; put into cold water and salt, and boil slowly five or six hours; skim well and add celery, onions, carrots and a few cloves; a little sage; let the meat be covered; brown the gravy with burned flour or sugar.
      MRS. CHAS. CULLIS, Boston.

GREEN PEA POD SOUP.

Wash the pods clean; cover with water and put on to boil about three hours; strain off the pods through the cullender and thicken the soup with flour and butter rubbed together; season with salt and pepper. Have in the tureen some pieces of bread well toasted and cut in small squares, pour the soup over and serve hot; a few of the green peas cooked in is a great addition.   MAGGIE FANNING.

MUTTON BROTH.

When you have mutton boiled for dinner, set the water it has been boiled in away to cool. The next day an hour or so before dinner, skim off the cake of grease that will be found on top; put the broth on to cook and season with a good deal of salt, little pepper; thicken with rice or barley.
Mrs. C. T. Richards.

CORN SOUP.

Take one dozen ears of good sweet corn; grate or scrape the corn from the ears; put cobs and corn into four quarts of cold water with a good sized chicken cut up, or two pounds of veal; boil two hours, then take out the corn cobs; add one quart or more of sweet milk; let it boil up, then thicken with a large spoonful of butter mixed smooth with a little flour; add pepper and salt to taste.

SOUP A LA REINE.

Seven pounds shank of veal; cold water enough to cover; after skimming add six large onions, cut in pieces; handful of green parsley; white pepper, not ground fine, but broken a little. After it is thoroughly boiled, strain through a sieve. Take off the grease from the top and return to the kettle; then add one pint and a half of cream; two tablespoonfuls of flour in the cream; and when it comes to a boil, it is ready to serve. Cook in a porcelain kettle; for eight persons.
Mrs. Cornelius Beer.

CORN CHOWDER.

Take ten ears of green corn, cut from cob; prepare potatoes in slices, as for fish chowder; place in a kettle alternate layers of each; season each layer with butter, pepper and salt; put in a pint of water; let it boil till the potatoes are cooked; add one quart of milk; thicken with a little flour; add crackers soaked in milk. Boil up once altogether.

DUMPLINGS.

Take a small teacupful of flour, a pinch of salt; rub in them a good teaspoonful of butter; add sweet milk enough to form a stiff dough; roll very thin; cut in small squares; drop into the soup and boil about ten minutes.

NOODLES.

Take one or two eggs, according to the quantity required; beat up light, add a little salt; then stir in flour until stiff; roll out thin as possible; let it stand to dry for thirty minutes or more; after drying dredge with flour; roll up close as you would a sheet of music; cut off shreds as thin as possible; shake them apart and let them dry a while; boil in the soup about twenty minutes.

FISH.

TO BOIL FISH.

Fish should be scaled and thoroughly cleaned, well salted, and put in a cold place till time to cook.

Boil in a fish kettle, with water enough to cover it, or wrap and tie in a cloth, and boil in any cooking vessel; if the fish is too large, it can be doubled in the cloth; cover with more than two inches of boiling water, adding a teaspoonful of salt and a tablespoonful of vinegar to every pound of fish. A good sized fish will cook in half an hour. Be careful not to break in taking it out.

SAUCE. Stir into a pint of boiling milk, a piece of butter the size of an egg, mixed with flour; and a hard boiled egg, cut up fine; pour this over the fish, or serve in a sauce-boat.
MRS. O. D. FILLEY.

FRIED FISH.

Having cleaned the fish thoroughly, wipe dry; score it on the back, in deep incisions or gashes; and slightly dredge with flour, pepper and salt. Be sure to have the lard boiling before the fish is put into it. MARY COLBURT.

BAKED FISH.

Clean and wipe the fish dry; tie a string round the head; and dredge with flour, pepper and salt; bake in a pan with butter and lard; and baste it often while baking; a good sized fish should cook in three quarters of an hour. If desired it can be stuffed with the same dressing used for turkeys, only more highly seasoned.
MRS. J. T. DAVIS.

FISH.

A very nice way to prepare fish. This makes an ornamental dish for the table. Take Cusk or Halibut; boil it; make it fine; add sufficient cream or melted butter to make it quite moist; flavor with grated lemon peel, a very little nutmeg, salt and pepper, with mashed potatoes; place the fish on the platter and ornament the top with beaten white of one egg; let it stand in the oven long enough to heat through; a little parsley and sliced lemon improves the dish. Mrs. Wm. Claflin, Boston.

STEWED FISH.

Fry two or three large onions; have the fish washed, dried, peppered, floured and salted; put the fish in with the onions and cook brown; add a little good stock and let it stew, add a spoonful of Harvey sauce.
Mrs. C. Cullis.

CUSK A LA CREME.

A fish weighing from two to three pounds; Cod, Blue fish or Halibut will do; rub well with salt and put in a kettle with enough water to cover it; when it comes to a boil set it where it will cool; when cool enough take out the bones; take one pint of milk or cream and boil one onion and a piece of mace in it; work smoothly a quarter of a pound of butter with some flour; stir into the milk until it thickens, making a smooth sauce by straining; add a little pepper; lay the fish on a deep dish and pour the sauce over it; sift crumbs over the top. Bake from half to three quarters of an hour. Mrs. Chas. Cullis, Boston.

TURBOT A LA CREME.

Put in a pudding dish layers of cooked fish, picked over, and bread crumbs, with a little finely chopped onion; black pepper, salt and butter. Beat up an egg in sufficient milk to come to the top layer. Bake about half an hour.

SCALLOPED LOBSTER.

Butter a deep dish; cover the bottom and sides with fine crumbs of bread; put in a layer of chopped boiled lobster, with pepper and a little salt; cover with crumbs and a little butter; add another layer of lobster, pepper and salt; cover as before; put in the liquor of the lobster; bake about twenty minutes. A good substitute for oysters in warm weather. MRS. JOSEPH STORY, Boston.

LOBSTER FARSEE.

Chop the Lobster fine; add a small lump of butter, half a cup of cream or milk, salt and pepper; make into small cakes; put a piece of butter on each cake; bake twenty minutes.

FISH PUDDING.

Take three pounds of fresh Cod or any other white fish; boil in the evening and after cooking take out the bones and mince quite fine; in the morning make a drawn butter sauce of one pint of milk, three eggs, a little flour, butter, salt and pepper; boil all together and mix with the fish; put all in a pudding dish and bake half an hour.

FISH SAUCE.

Beat a teacup of butter to a cream; add a little French and English mustard, the juice of one lemon and chopped cucumber pickle.

FRESH FISH WARMED OVER.

One pint of fish picked fine, one quart of milk, two eggs, one-fourth of a cup of flour, mixed with a little of the milk; pepper, salt and nutmeg, one-fourth of a teaspoonful each. Mix smoothly the milk, flour, eggs and spice. Set this sauce over the fire and stir until thick as cream. Put in a deep dish alternately, the sauce, fish and bread crumbs in the order mentioned; brown lightly in the oven.

MRS. KRUM.

COD FISH.

Pick to pieces a pint of Cod fish and soak it over night; if not sufficiently fresh, pour cold water over it and let it come to a boil; after turning off the water, add half a pint of milk or cream; a dessertspoonful of butter; when thoroughly cooked add four eggs.

COD FISH RELISH.

One cup salt Cod fish shredded fine; three cups hot water, two soda crakers broken small; butter size of a walnut; one cup of milk; boil all together.

MRS. S. A. RANLETT.

COD FISH BALLS.

Cut the fish in pieces; put to soak in a saucepan with the skin side up; put on the fire; change the water two or three times; let the water come to a scald (but not boil); when soft take the fish out; skin it; take out the bones; chop very fine; have twice as much mashed potatoes as fish; mix together with a little milk and butter; mould into small cakes and fry.

FISH BALLS.

One pint dry Cod fish, picked to pieces; one quart potatoes peeled and sliced; wash the fish, but not soak it; put them in a pan together and boil till the potatoes are done; drain off the water; mash them up together; add two eggs well beaten; piece of butter the size of an egg; make them into balls, and fry immediately.

C. G. HILL.

OYSTERS.

In using oysters raw always buy the largest you can, and if you are going to serve oysters in more than one way, it is best to pick out the largest from all the cans for raw, or fried; in soups and other things it does not make so much difference about the size. Raw oysters must be served alone, with the best of wine or cider vinegar, mustard, salt and pepper passed around. Lemons are cut in pieces about one-eighth large, lengthwise, with the skins left on, so that those who like can squeeze the juice out easily.

RAW OYSTERS.

The following is a handsome way to serve raw oysters: Take a nice clear square piece of ice, about ten pounds, and with *hot* flat irons *melt* out a deep dish in the middle of the ice, leaving an edge about one inch wide all around to keep in the oysters, it is not at all necessary to keep the inside edge straight or square, for the more jagged it is the prettier it will look; while doing it I keep two or three irons heating on the stove. Have a large platter covered with a napkin, and set the block of ice in it; (the base may be decorated with parsley or celery tops at will,) then put in your oysters and they will get just cold enough to be nice. It must not be fixed too long before serving. The platter will catch all the water that melts from the ice.

MRS. E. F. RICHARDS.

FRIED OYSTERS.

Wipe dry one can of oysters; beat up two eggs; season with pepper and salt; dip in the oysters, and roll them in cracker flour; have hot lard in a pan, and fry them quickly in it.

MARY COLBURT.

OYSTERS.

FRIED OYSTERS.

Use for frying the largest oysters. Drain from them all the juice; take some soda crackers and roll them with the rolling pin on the bread board or table; when fine, season with plenty of salt and pepper; have ready several beaten eggs; dip the oyster first in the egg then roll in the fine crumbs until covered thick; have ready in your frying pan some hot lard or butter; drop one oyster in first to see if hot enough; fry quickly and turn when brown and don't let them remain in the fat one instant after done. Serve dry on a warm dish.

FRICASSEED OYSTERS.

Put two cans of oysters in a stew pan and let them come to a boil; then strain them out and lay them on a dish; have ready one tablespoonful of flour, two of butter, a little salt and pepper; stir well together, and pour in the liquor and let it boil for a few moments, stirring carefully; then put in the oysters, and when come to a boil pour over buttered toast.   MRS. FRANK FILLEY.

STEWED OYSTERS.

To half a can of fresh oysters poured into a stew pan, add about an ounce of butter; half a tablespoonful of flour, previously stirred with a small quantity of milk; when nearly to the boiling point, add milk to taste and boil for two minutes.   MRS. LEWIS E. KLINE.

SCALLOPED OYSTERS.

One can of oysters; one-half dozen soda crackers, rolled fine; fill the dish with successive layers of crackers and oysters; seasoning the oysters with pepper, salt, and little pieces of butter; pour the liquid over the top. Bake in quick oven for three quarters of an hour.
        MARY COLBURT.

SCALLOPED OYSTERS.

Put the oysters in their own liquor over the fire, let them come to a boil over a slow fire, then lay the oysters in a buttered dish with alternate layers of cracker crumbs, a little butter and pepper; put cracker crumbs on top and brown them in the oven; take care not to let them cook long enough to dry, and not have the layers of crackers too thick.

OYSTERS ON TOAST.

Take a can of *select* oysters; drain off the liquor through a cullender. Take one pint of milk and one pint of cream, or one quart of cream; put it into a sauce pan, and when it comes to a boil, add one tablespoonful of corn starch, previously wet in cold water; piece of butter size of an egg, and salt and pepper. When this boils, add the oysters, cooking them only long enough to make the lips curl. Toast enough bread, cutting off the crust, to fill an ordinary size vegetable dish. When all is done, put into the dish first a layer of toast and then a layer of oysters.

Mrs. J. G. Chapman.

STEWED OYSTERS.

Open your cans and drain the juice from the oysters; mix with the juice a little hot water; add salt and pepper and put in a stew pan on the fire; when it comes to a boil add more than a cup full of cream or milk. Let it come to a boil, being careful not to burn, then add the oysters and two spoonfuls of butter well stirred in; let them boil five minutes, no longer; serve in a hot tureen. Have oyster crackers to eat with them.

OYSTER SOUP.

Drain the juice from a can or quart of oysters; put on the stove and to it add one-half pint of water, one large cracker rolled very fine; pepper, salt and a good bit of butter; when the juice is scalded drop in the oysters and cook until the lips curl, when they are done.

Mrs. C. B. Richards.

OYSTER SOUP.

Take one quart of oysters and separate them from the liquor; wash them thoroughly in a pint of water. Strain the liquor, add one pint of milk, some mace, nutmeg and pepper, with three crackers pounded fine; add one-fourth pound of butter; boil all together about five minutes; take it off the fire. When about to serve up the soup, put in the oysters and let it boil one minute, and the soup will be ready for the table. For each quart of oysters a pint of milk must be added and every other ingredient in proportion. Three pints of oysters are sufficient for eight persons.

MRS. T. T. RICHARDS.

OYSTER PIE.

Have your oysters cooked as for stewed oyters, only add a little more thickening of craker crumbs and the yolks of two or three eggs beaten up very light. Line a deep dish with a rich pie paste and fill it with white paper, napkin or anything that will hold up the top of the pie; put on the cover and bake in a quick oven a light brown. When done take off the lid; take out the white paper or napkin and pour in the half stewed oysters; set back in the oven a few moments and serve hot. Oyster patties are made in the same manner only the crust is baked in small tin patty-pans which come for that purpose, and they can have covers or not just as you choose, they look equally well without; some like a little nutmeg grated over them, and some a little lemon juice squeezd in.

PICKLE OYSTERS.

Fish out the oysters with a fork; put them on to stew with salt to season them; pour them in a cullender to drain; then make a strong salt and water to wash them in; after being washed perfectly clean, put them in a stone jar. Strain the liquor in which they were stewed through a cloth; add spices, about one tablespoonful of black pepper, mace, allspice, cloves and a little ginger; put it on the fire and boil until the liquor is well flavored; then when about milk-warm pour to the oysters and let stand twenty-four hours; then add vinegar to your taste. This quantity of spice is for a gallon.

MEATS.

TIME FOR COOKING SUNDRIES.

TIME GIVEN TO ROASTING ALL KINDS OF MEAT IS A QUARTER OF AN HOUR TO A POUND, AND THE SAME FOR BOILING.

BOILED MEATS.

Fresh meats should always be cooked in boiling water and kept constantly boiling, if not, the meat will soak up the water. If more water is needed be careful that it is boiling water; remove the scum when it first begins to boil; allow twenty minutes for each pound of fresh meat. Salt meats should be boiled in cold water, allowing twenty-four minutes to every pound. The more gently meat boils the more tender it is.

ROAST BEEF.

The best cuts are the tenderloin, and first and second rib cuts. Sprinkle the roast with salt and pepper, and dredge with a little flour; pour a little water in the pan to be used for basting; allow one quarter of an hour to the pound for rare meat; longer if to be well done. When the meat is done remove to a hot platter, and then pour off the fat and thicken the gravy with flour that has been first rubbed to a smooth paste in a little water; season it with salt and pepper if necessary. Beef is better in winter when kept from two to four weeks.

BEEF STEAK.

A porter house steak one inch thick is considered the best cut for a steak, the next best is a sirloin. Trim them nicely; many persons prefer their steaks well pounded; sprinkle with salt and pepper; lay it on the gridiron; put over clear hot coals, turning over it a pan in order to keep the steam in; turn it frequently, but be careful not to stick the fork in to let the juice escape. As soon as the steak is done put it on a warm plate with a lump of butter, press the steak with a knife on both sides so as to extract the juice.

Mrs. C——.

YORKSHIRE PUDDING.

One quart of sweet milk, four eggs, six tablespoonfuls of flour, a little salt, and I generally put in a very little of soda. To be cooked in the gravy of roast beef.

Put the pudding into the oven and bake for an hour, then for another half hour place it under the meat to catch a little of the gravy that flows from it. Cut the pudding into small square pieces, put them on a hot dish and serve. If the meat is baked the pudding may at once be placed under it resting the former on a small three-cornered stand.

Mrs. J. B. Flintham.

FILLET OF VEAL.

Take six pounds of the leg of veal; have the bone taken out. With a sharp knife make gashes through the thick part of the meat. Make a dressing of chopped raw salt pork, pepper, sweet herbs and bread crumbs, or use butter instead of pork; fill in the gashes and the hole from which the bone was taken; sew up, and tie tightly in a round roll. Put into a pan with a pint of water, baste it thoroughly, and bake for two hours.

ROAST VEAL.

The loin is the best for roasting. Wash the piece to be roasted in cold water, sprinkle a little salt and pepper over it; put a pint of water in the pan, and baste often with the drippings. Veal should be cooked very thoroughly.

FORCE MEAT BALLS.

Half a pound of veal, half a pound of suet chopped fine, a few sweet herbs and parsley cut fine, a little pounded mace and a small nutmeg, a little lemon peel grated, pepper and salt, the yolks of two eggs; mix all of them well together, then roll them into small round balls, roll them in flour and fry them brown. If they are for anything white, put a little water in a saucepan, and when the water boils put them in and let them boil for a few minutes.
MRS. SAM'L TREAT.

TO BOIL A LEG OF VEAL.

Put the meat in boiling water, with a few slices of pork in it. When done make a gravy of drawn butter. Time for cooking two to three hours.

VEAL CUTLET.

The nicest cutlets are from the round; about half an inch thick; season with salt and pepper; dip into beaten egg, then in flour. Put into a skillet with hot lard, and fry a nice brown. When done, take out, make a gravy with a little flour and water.

HAUNCH OF VENISON.

Take the venison, wash and dry well; butter a sheet of white paper, and cover it over the venison; then cover with two or three more thicknesses of strong paper, tied on with strong twine; put into the pan, and as soon as in the oven baste the paper well and constantly to keep from burning; about thirty minutes before being done, which can be told by running a skewer in, and if tender, 'tis done; remove the papers, and dredge the meat with flour and baste with butter, until a nice brown color. Must be served on very hot plates, and currant jelly passed around.

VENISON STEAKS.

Lay the steak on a gridiron over a clear, hot fire; turn quickly; season with salt, pepper and a little butter; generally liked quite rare.

TO CORN BEEF.

To fifty pounds of meat, ten pounds coarse salt, two pounds brown sugar, two ounces of saltpetre; rub the meat well with the mixture, and add water enough to corn the meat. Mrs. Cornelia Beer.

CORN BEEF.

To fifty pounds beef, three and a half gallons water, ten pounds fine salt, one and a half pounds brown sugar, one ounce saltpetre; rub into the beef a little salt and let it stand a few days until the blood is drawn out; move the blood away: pack the beef in a cask; scald the brine, skim, and when cold pour over the beef. It will be fit for use in ten days or a fortnight. Mrs. Rhodes.

BOILED CORN BEEF.

Take either the blade or round of beef, let your butcher take out all the bones and roll it, tie it round with broad strong tape; put it into a large pot; cover it well with cold water; carefully take off the scum as it rises; when no more appears, keep the pot closely covered; let it boil slowly. Allow three hours and a half to a piece weighing about twelve pounds; turn the meat twice in the pot while it is boiling. When done it is very nice to press it by putting it in a stone crock, putting a plate on top with a heavy weight; let it stand until cold.

BOILED SMOKED TONGUE.

Soak over night in cold water; in the morning put on to boil in cold water, cooking slowly three or four hours. When done skin it and moisten with the yolk of an egg; roll it in bread crumbs; place in the oven until light brown.

Garnish the dish with parsley or celery, and serve hot. To be eaten with boiled turkey; or when the tongue is boiled, skin while hot, and when cold cut in thin slices and place neatly on a platter. MRS. LASHELLS.

BOILED MUTTON.

To boil mutton, put it in cold water; add a little salt; skim well. A leg weighing six or eight pounds will boil in two hours. Serve with a gravy made of drawn butter, season with capers or mint.

COLD SADDLE OF MUTTON.

ENGLISH MODE OF DRESSING.

Time, eleven minutes. Cold saddle of mutton; one spoonful of chopped onions; one ounce of butter; one tablespoonful of flour; one teaspoonful of pepper and salt mixed; a little cayenne; half a pint of broth; one bay leaf; two eggs; two pounds and a half of mashed potatoes. Cut out all the meat remaining on a cold saddle of mutton close to the bone, leaving an edge of about an inch and a half wide outside; chop the meat small with a little of the fat. Put a dessertspoonful of chopped onions into a stew pan with a little butter, fry them for one minute; add the meat, sprinkle over it a tablespoonful of flour; season it rather high; moisten it with half a pint of broth, and put a bay leaf in the gravy; stew the whole for ten minutes, then add the beaten yolks of two eggs; stir it till it is rather thick. Mash two pounds of potatoes very stiffly, so that they will form a paste; roll them out; form an edging with them round the saddle of mutton; fill the empty space in the joint with the mince. If you have not meat enough to fill up the hollow, add any minced cold remains of other joints, provided they are mutton; egg and bread crumb the saddle all over; put it in rather a hot oven to brown. Serve with Espagnole sauce.

BOILED LAMB.

Take a round of lamb, boil two or three hours in water seasoned with salt and pepper. Make a dressing of egg sauce, with chopped parsley. Serve with currant jelly. Side dishes with boiled lamb are asparagus or peas, potatoes and lettuce.   MRS. E. R. L.

ROAST LAMB.

The fore and hind quarters of lamb are used for roasting. Sprinkle it with a little salt and pepper, and a little flour; put it in the pan with a little water; baste it frequently. Lamb must be thoroughly cooked. It is very nice to make a dressing of bread crumbs, butter, pepper and salt, with a very little sage or thyme; lay this on the ribs, covering with the flap, and sew firmly, to keep it in its place.

ROAST LOIN OF PORK.

Score the skin in narrow strips; rub it all over with powdered sage leaves, pepper and salt. Have ready a dressing of minced onions and sage, bread crumbs and the yolk of one egg, salt and pepper. Make deep incisions between the ribs, and fill them with the dressing. You may roast in the same way a shoulder, spare rib, or chine of pork, seasoning it with sage and onion. Have ready some apple sauce to eat with the pork.

SPARE RIB OF PORK ROASTED.

Joint it down the middle, and sprinkle with fine sage and salt; baste and flour well. Serve with apple sauce.

SAUSAGE.

Four and one-half ounces salt; one ounce of sage; one ounce pepper; ten pounds of meat.
     MRS. W. MAURICE.

SAUSAGE MEAT.

Two pounds fresh, lean pork, or beef, raw; one pound fat salt pork; three teaspoonfuls of pepper; nine teaspoonfuls of sage. Chop very fine; mix thoroughly; roll into small flat cakes, and fry; but do not put any fat in the pan.

BOILED HAM.

Wash a ham well in soap suds and rinse in clean water; let it soak over night; in the morning put it on to boil in cold water, letting it simmer an hour, then boil slowly for three or four hours; when done take it out and remove the skin and place it in the oven a short time. If you wish it warm for dinner spread with bread crumbs mixed with a little sage and return to oven to brown; stick into it some whole cloves and garnish the dish with pastry or celery.

BAKED HAM.

Cover the ham with a paste of flour and water; while cooking baste it with either cider, rhine or sherry wine diluted with water; when done remove the paste and skin from the ham; then sprinkle with rolled cracker and return to the oven to brown. MRS. WM. MAURICE.

BAKED HAMS.

Soak the ham for an hour in clear water and wipe it dry; next spread it all over with thin batter, and then put it into a deep dish with sticks under it to keep it out of the gravy; when it is fully done, take off the skin and batter crushed upon the flesh side, and set it away to cool.

MRS. LEWIS E. KLINE.

TO BROIL HAM.

Cut the ham in thin slices; soak them in hot water ten or fifteen minutes; dry them in a cloth and lay them over a hot gridiron and broil a few minutes. Butter and season with a little pepper. MRS. LEWIS E. KLINE.

POTTED BEEF.

Take three pounds of lean beef, put it on to boil covered with water; let it simmer until perfectly tender, when it will be easily chopped; chop it in a wooden bowl; then pound it in a marble mortar or bowl, adding gradually the liquor in which the meat was boiled; some nice marrow from the beef bones should be added before the meat is done, but if you have no marrow add a little melted butter as you pound. Season it with pepper and salt to taste, with a little cloves, allspice and grated nutmeg may be added. When finely pounded put it in small jars, press it down, and the next day cover it with melted butter which will preserve it much longer than if left open. Veal may be done in the same way, omitting spices except mace.

BEEF A LA MODE.

Take a round of fresh beef and beat it well to make it tender. Rub it all over with salt and pepper, lard it on both sides with bacon; put a calf's foot, a few onions, a carrot cut in pieces, a bunch of sweet herbs cut small, one or two laurel leaves, some cloves and a beaten nutmeg in the pan. Pour in a half a pint of red wine and a half a pint of white wine, a spoonful of brandy. Let it stew slowly six hours; take it out and strain the gravy; pour it on the meat and serve. Venison is very nice done in the same way; both are better prepared the night before.

SPICED BEEF.

Purchase of your butcher a round of beef of twelve or sixteen pounds weight; let it lay in salt two hours; take it out; wash clean; rub with salt and saltpetre until very red; then take a tablespoonful each of allspice, mace and black pepper; mix them with the marrow which comes out of the bone; let it lay nine days in this mixture, turning and rubbing it every day; then tie it closely in a cloth and steam it by the following process. Put your vessel for cooking it over the fire with a quart of water; place some sticks in the vessel and lay your meat upon it; renew the water whenever it evaporates. Steam three hours or until you can put a fork through it. This dish is highly esteemed in the south for lunches. To be eaten cold.　　　　MRS. WELLS.

HASH.

Take cold beef of any kind; chop fine; then take about one-third mashed potatoes; season with salt and pepper; very little water. It is also very nice to leave out the potatoes; have some slices of bread toasted, laid on the platter, and pour the meat on the toast.

MEAT PIE.

Cut up meat in slices; season with salt, pepper, onion and parsley; cover with tomatoes and bread crumbs; butter on top.

TO WARM COLD MEATS.

Chop the meat fine; add salt, pepper, a little onion and tomato catsup; fill a baking dish one-third full, cover it over with boiled potatoes mashed with milk; lay bits of butter on top, and bake fifteen or twenty minutes.

MYSTERY.

Take any kind of cold meat chopped fine, with cold ham or salt pork; season with salt and pepper, and mix in two eggs and a little butter; mix this with rusk crumbs, and bake like pudding or put in a skillet and warm like hash, or put into balls, flatten and fry like sausages.

BEEF OMELET.

Two pounds raw beef chopped fine; one egg well beaten, two crackers pounded fine; piece of butter size of one-half an egg melted. Pepper, salt and sage to taste; mix well together with a little flour on kneading board. Bake one hour in pan with a little water; baste often; slice when cold.

FRIED BEEF STEAK or LAMB CHOPS.

Pound and sprinkle well with flour; season with salt and pepper; lay in a frying pan with hot lard or butter; turn frequently until done.   Mrs. G. R. W.

BEEF STEAK SMOTHERED IN ONIONS.

Slice your onions; lay them in the skillet; cover with pieces of butter, pepper and salt; put in your steak, then another layer of onions; cover tight; cook slowly two hours.

BEEF PIE.

Take small pieces of beef, put them in a pot with water enough to cover; boil slowly two hours, keeping tightly covered. When half done have some raw potatoes sliced very thin, and a few thin pieces of salt pork. Line the sides of your dish with a plain pie crust; putting an inverted teacup in the middle to absorb the juice, then fill round the dish with a layer of meat; then potatoes seasoned with salt, pepper, cloves, a few sliced onions if liked, and a few pieces of pork; so on until your dish is full; pour in as much of the liquor the meat was boiled in as will almost fill the dish; put an upper crust on, making a slit in the middle and picking it with a fork, then put it in the oven to bake. Always in making meat pies of any kind be very particular and cut the slit in the upper crust, in order to let the gas and steam escape while cooking. Veal or mutton cooked in same manner is very nice.   Mrs. S. T. Glover.

FRIZZLED BEEF.

Chip dried beef; put in a pan with some hot water; let it come to a boil; pour that water off; add a little milk thickened with a very little flour, a lump of butter and a little pepper, let it come to a boil; serve hot.

MOCK DUCK.

Take a flank steak; make a dressing the same as for ducks; spread it on the steak; then roll and tie tight with a string to keep the roll in shape; lay it in a pan with a little water; sprinkle with pepper and salt; put in the oven to bake. MRS. T. P. SAUNDERS.

SAVORY BEEF.

Take a shin of beef from the hind quarter; saw it into four pieces; put it in a pot and boil until the meat and gristle drop from the bones; chop the meat very fine; put it into a dish or jar and season with salt, pepper, cloves and sage to your taste; pour in the liquor in which the meat was boiled and place away to harden. Cut in slices and eat cold.
MRS. BROCK.

BROILED MUTTON CHOPS.

Take chops or steaks from a loin of mutton; beat them to make them tender, season with pepper and salt; put them on a gridiron hot over a bed of clear bright coals; turn them frequently; when done put them into a warm dish and butter them. When the chops have been turned for the last time you may strew over them some minced onion moistened with boiling water; season with pepper. Some like them flavored with mushroom catsup.

Another way of dressing mutton chops is, after trimming nicely and seasoning with pepper and salt, lay them for a while in melted butter; when they have imbibed a sufficient quantity take them out; cover all over with grated bread crumbs; broil them over a clear fire and see that the bread does not burn.

IRISH STEW.

Take mutton chops, cover well with water; let come to a boil; pour off this and add more water. Take a lump of butter the size of an egg; two tablespoonfuls of flour, a teacup of milk with pepper and salt to taste, also a few potatoes, a small onion or two, if liked. Boil all until the potatoes are done.

LIVER DAUB.

Take a liver and put it on the fire in cold water, with one teaspoonful of vinegar; let it come to a boil, then take it out and lay in cold water to clean it. Lard it with fat pork, and dredge flour over it. Take one good tablespoonful of lard and melt it; have some onions cut very fine, and fry it in the lard; then put in the liver and let it fry a little on both sides; then add sliced carrots, and one pint of broth, and let it stew about an hour; as the broth boils away add more; pepper, salt and spice to your taste.

MRS. CORNELIA BEER.

CALF LIVER.

Cut into slices one-half inch thick; place in a pan with hot lard enough to keep from sticking. When done take out; make a gravy by adding a little water, flour salt and pepper.

CALF'S HEAD.

Put in the head to soak the day before; split it open, take out the brains, pick it clean, tie it in a bag; take out the eyes, put the head and the lights and heart on to boil, and boil two hours; the liver one hour; put the brains on to boil with the liver, put in a little butter, pepper, sage and salt, and a little flour if not thick enough, set it on the stove, and let it boil up a little; take part of the liver, lights and head, chop it fine; then take a little of the liquor out of the pot, and put in butter, pepper, sage and salt, and a little pounded cracker, and heat it on the stove; take up the head and take out the loose bones, and the best of the liver, lights and heart and put them in a dish for the table; put the brain sauce in a gravy tureen, and the hash in a covered dish. What is left after dinner, hash it all together, and the next day warm it over, putting in pepper, salt, sage and butter, the same as the day before. If there is any left after this, put it in a pan, and you can cut in slices cold for breakfast, like head-cheese.

MRS. N. R. HILL.

SAUSAGE MEAT.

Seven pounds of lean meat, five pounds of back bone fat, seven tablespoonfuls of sage, five of salt and three of pepper.   Mrs. Frank A. Lane.

TO DRESS BEEF KIDNEY.

Soak a fresh kidney in cold water and dry in a cloth; cut it in pieces and chop fine; dust it with flour; put some butter into a saucepan over a moderate fire; when it boils put in the minced kidney; when browned in the butter, sprinkle a little salt and cayenne pepper; pour in a very little boiling water; add a glass of champagne or other wine, or a large teaspoonful of mushroom catsup or of walnut pickle; cover the pan closely; let it stew until the kidney is tender; send to the table hot. It is generally eaten for breakfast.

FRIED KIDNEY.

Lay the kidney in salt and water half an hour; take out and cut in thin slices; roll a few oyster crackers very fine; beat an egg light; dip the kidney in the egg, then in the cracker; have some hot lard in the frying pan; lay the kidney in and sprinkle with salt, pepper and fine cut parsley; pour in a few spoonfuls of boiling water; cook until a fork can be run through easily; then set in the oven and brown nicely.   Miss L. D.

STEWED KIDNEY.

Cut the kidney in small pieces; cook in boiling water ten minutes or until the water is nearly boiled away; sprinkle with salt and pepper; rub together one tablespoonful of flour, butter size of half an egg with a few spoonfuls of cream or new milk, a little parsley cut fine; boil until the gravy thickens and pour it over a slice or two of toast.
    Miss L. D.

TRIPE.

Procure from your butcher a tripe ready dressed; soak in salt and water twenty-four hours; cut in four or five pieces; put in a tin kettle with cold water; let it simmer three or four hours, skimming it well; change the water adding a handful of salt; boil five or six hours or until quite tender, try it with a fork. When done remove from the kettle; take one or two of the best pieces; sprinkle with pepper, salt, a little cinnamon and mace; roll up tight, tie with a strong string; lay away to get cold; cut the remainder in pieces from four to six inches; place them in a stone jar with pepper, cinnamon, mace and very little cloves; pour good vinegar over; it will then be ready for use. In the morning slice the rolls half an inch thick; place in the jar with the other. This can be eaten cold.   MRS. LASHELLS.

TRIPE AND OYSTERS.

Take a piece of tripe after it has been boiled and cut it in small pieces. Put it in a saucepan with just milk enough to cover it and a few pieces of mace; let it boil a few moments, then put in your oysters, a large piece of butter rolled in flour, salt, pepper to taste. Let it boil a few minutes longer; send it to the table; if any fat rises to the surface skim it off.

TO FRY TRIPE.

Take what you wish to use out of the vinegar; dip in beaten egg, then in bread crumbs or flour; season if necessary; fry in a pan in butter and lard until a nice brown; make the gravy with flour water; a little vinegar or what is better, some mushroom or walnut catsup.

     MRS. L.

TRIPE AND OYSTERS.

Take boiled tripe, cut it up into small pieces; put it in a saucepan with just milk enough to cover it and a few blades of mace; let it stew about five minutes; then put in the oysters; adding a large piece of butter rolled in flour; salt and cayenne pepper to taste; let it stew about five minutes longer. Send it to the table in a covered dish, first skimming off whatever fat may float on the surface.

HAM SANDWICHES.

Chop or grate fine some cold boiled ham; mix with a little chopped pickle, or juice of a lemon; one teaspoonful of mustard, and a little pepper; mix these together; butter four slices of bread and spread the dressed ham on them; place the slices together. The chopped pickle can be omitted if not desired. MRS. M. E. G.

ENGLISH BEEF AND POTATO SANDWICH.

EIGHT OR TEN MINUTES.

Some slices of salt beef; yolks of eggs; bread crumbs; some mashed potatoes. Fry some slices of cold salt beef very lightly, when done spread very evenly over each side a thick layer of mashed potatoes, press it over them with the blade of a knife, and then cover them with egg and bread crumbs; fry them in boiling fat a fine brown; serve very hot.

HOW TO COOK A LEG OF MUTTON.

Select a fat juicy joint; salt and pepper well; let it lie two or three days if the weather is cold, if warm twenty-four hours in the ice chest; then wash clean; boil from two to three hours, according to the size and age of the mutton; throw in a pod or part of a pod of red pepper while boiling; when sufficiently boiled put the joint in the dripping pan; have some crumbs of bread seasoned with a little sage; sear the joint slightly, put in the dressing and roast until brown, basting it well. The sage is optional to to the taste.

MRS. T. B. EDGAR.

VEAL OMELET.

Three pounds raw veal; four slices salt pork chopped fine; three eggs, two tablespoonfuls cream or milk, four powdered crackers; season with sage or thyme; one teaspoonful pepper, one of salt, one-half nutmeg; form into a loaf and bake two or three hours in a slow oven; baste with butter and water; cut in very thin slices for the table.

Mrs. R. H. Morton.

BEEF LOAF.

Three pounds of lean beef; three eggs; six Boston crackers rolled; salt and pepper; a little cream and melted butter; cloves and nutmeg. Mix well and bake in a loaf for an hour.

WELTON VEAL.

Boil four eggs hard, slice them and line a dish; then place a layer of raw veal, cut thin. Mix chopped ham with one egg and sage for next layer; then another of veal and so on till the dish is full. Cover with a flat cover; put weight on top to press; steam four hours. To be eaten cold cut in thin slices.

VEAL LOAF.

Three and a half pounds of the finest part of the lean and fat of a leg of veal, chopped very fine; three common sized crackers, rolled fine; two eggs; a piece of butter size of an egg; a teaspoonful of salt, one of pepper, and grated nutmeg; a thick slice of salt pork, chopped fine. Mix all together; bake in a tin bread pan; put bits of butter and grated bread crumbs over it, and bake two hours. Put a little water in another pan, and set this in it; bake slowly. To be eaten when cold, cut in thin slices. Mrs. T. T. Richards.

VEAL OMELET.

Take three pounds of veal chopped fine; three eggs well beaten; six small butter crackers, rolled fine; two tablespoonfuls pepper, one of sage. Mix all well together; add bits of butter to the taste; form into a loaf and bake two hours, basting often. Mrs. Lewis E. Kline.

MEATS.

RICHAMELLA.

Mince your cold roast veal in a chopping bowl; leave out the stringy part; put into the frying pan a teacupful or more of milk or sweet cream, into which stir, when hot, a tablespoonful of butter and flour, well mixed together; then add veal. Heat it well through; grate a little nutmeg or fine mace over. Delicious for breakfast; can be used for veal patties. MRS. D. YOUNG.

VEAL FRICANDEAU.

Take a small fillet without a bone, lard it well with pork, putting it into the meat where there is no skin; butter the chafing-dish (some people lay a slice or two of bacon in the dish), put the meat in larded side up, place therein four carrots, four onions, a bunch of parsley, thyme or marjoram, two or three cloves, two glasses of water, and a little pepper. If the piece weigh three or four pounds, it must stew for three hours gently, covered close. Before serving take out the carrots and onions, baste the meat well with the gravy, take off all the fat, add to it a spoonful of brown flour and one glass of wine, stir it well in and pour it over the meat; to serve it add to the gravy either tomato ketchup, sorrel or spinach as you choose.
MRS. SAM'L TREAT.

VEAL OLIVES.

Slice as large pieces as you can get from a leg of veal; make a stuffing of grated bread, butter, a little onion minced, salt, pepper, and spread over the slices. Beat an egg and put over the stuffing. Roll each slice up tightly, and tie with a thread; stick a few cloves in them; grate bread thickly over them after being put in the skillet, with butter and onions chopped fine; when done lay them on a dish; make your gravy and pour over them; take the threads off, and garnish with eggs, boiled hard, and serve. To be cut in slices. MRS. U. S. GRANT.

STEW PIE OF VEAL.

Take a knuckle of veal and cut in pieces; when the water boils put them in and boil it for a half or three-quarters of an hour; then take out the meat and place on a dish; season the liquor with butter, pepper and salt; thicken with flour as you would for gravy; have your biscuit or balls very light and put them in when boiling; lay a cloth over the kettle, which do not uncover till boiled; time for cooking twenty minutes. J. R. A.

SWEET BREADS.

Choose large white sweet breads; put them in warm water for half an hour, then parboil them; when cold cut in pieces about three-quarters of an inch thick; dip in yolk of an egg, then in bread crumbs (some add spice, lemon peel and sweet herbs); put some clean drippings in a frying pan; when hot put in the sweet breads and fry a nice brown. For garnishing, crisp parsley, and for sauce, mushroom catsup and melted butter or anchovy sauce.

STEWED SWEET BREADS.

Soak the sweet breads in warm water half an hour; then boil ten minutes; take them out; put them in cold water for a few moments, then lay them in a saucepan and simmer gently for rather more than half an hour. Dish them; thicken the gravy with a little butter and flour, six tablespoonfuls of cream, one tablespoonful of lemon juice, one blade pounded mace, pepper and salt to taste; let it boil a few moments; pour over the sweet breads.

A PIE OF SWEET BREAD AND OYSTERS.

Boil the sweet breads tender; season with pepper and salt; make a gravy with the water in which they were boiled, adding half a cup of cream, butter size of an egg, the yolks of two eggs and a tablespoonful of flour. Line the bottom and sides of a dish with puff paste; have the same quantity of oysters as of sweet breads: lay the oysters in first, cover with sweet breads and fill the dish with gravy; place the crust on top and bake.

WELSH RAREBIT.

One pound cheese, two large tablespoonfuls of butter, one cup of cream, three eggs well beaten, cayenne and black pepper, little salt to taste: put cheese and butter into the oven until it melts, then stir in the milk and eggs, put back into the oven and bake like custard; let it get quite brown; when done pour over buttered toast.

Mrs. M. Saunders.

WELSH RAREBIT.

Cut your cheese in small slips if soft, if hard grate it; have ready a spirit lamp; put in the cheese with a lump of butter, and set it over the lamp; beat the yolk of an egg with half a glass of Madeira wine, and as much ale or beer; stir the cheese and butter until thoroughly mixed, then add gradually the egg and wine; keep stirring until it forms a smooth mass; season well with cayenne pepper and grated nutmeg. To be eaten with hot toast.

Mrs. R. H. Morton.

WELSH RAREBIT.

One pound of new cheese, add half pint of water; stew over a hot fire till melted; add one teaspoonful of mixed mustard, one teaspoonful olive oil, a little cayenne pepper; pour on the hot toast in a hot covered dish; serve at once.

Astor House.

ECONOMICAL CROQUETTES.

If you have veal soup for dinner, take the meat off the bone and mince it; to two cups of minced veal put two cups of stale bread soaked in water; then squeeze very dry; mix thoroughly with the minced veal; have a calf's brain boiled soft and mashed; mix with the rest, then season with salt, pepper, summer savory, sweet marjoram, a little butter or cream, yolk of an egg, the grated rind of one and juice of two lemons; mould in shape and brown in a skillet with hot lard. For those who like it, chopped parsley and a very little chopped onion is a great addition.

MRS. E. F. RICHARDS.

SWEET BREAD CROQUETTES.

Put the sweet breads to soak in luke-warm water (to draw out the blood), then boil them thoroughly, mash them and cut off the stringy part; prepare as much again bread crumbs; season with salt, pepper, summer savory, a little butter, mix all together, then mould in shape, fry in lard and a little butter to make them a nice brown.

MRS. E. F. RICHARDS.

SWEET BREAD.

Boil it half an hour, then throw it into cold water to plump out; roll it in eggs and bread crumbs, seasoned with salt and pepper; lay them in a pan, a lump of butter on each, and bake them. A nice gravy is made of veal stewed, seasoned and strained.

SWEET BREADS.

Scald them in salt and water, and take out the stringy parts; then put them in cold water for a few moments; dry them in a towel, dip in egg and crumbs, and fry brown in butter; when they are done, take them on a dish, pour into the frying pan a large cup of sweet cream, a little pepper and salt, and a little green parsley, chopped fine; dust in a very little flour, and when it boils up, pour it over the breads, and send to the table hot.

HAM TOAST.

Boil quarter of a pound of lean ham, chop fine and mix with the yolks of three beaten eggs; add one-half ounce butter, two tablespoonfuls cream and a little pepper; stir over

the fire until it thickens; cut the crust from some nice slices of bread, toast them and turn the ham over.
NANTUCKET.

TO USE UP BITS OF HAM.

Cut off all the fat, and mince very fine; break a half dozen fresh eggs into a pan, add a tablespoonful of cream, a little salt and pepper, and put over the fire; as soon as the eggs are set or nearly solid, spread one-half thickly with the minced ham and fold the other over it; slip it carefully from pan to dish. Garnish with parsley; serve hot.

PIGS' FEET AND EARS SOUSED.

Having cleaned them properly and removed the skin, boil them slowly till they are quite tender, then split the feet and put them with the ears into salt and vinegar flavored with a little mace; cover the jar closely and set it away. When you use them, dry each piece well with a cloth; dip them first in beaten yolk of egg, then in bread crumbs, and fry them nicely in butter or lard. Or they may be eaten cold out of the vinegar. If you intend keeping them some time, you must make a fresh pickle for them every other day.

PIGS' FEET.

Boil them until they are done thoroughly, then split the claw, and fry them in batter, just dipped into the batter.

Batter: one-half pint of milk, one egg, little salt; flour enough to make it a little thicker than flapjacks; fry them in hot fat.
C. G. HILL.

GRAVIES AND SAUCES.

After roasting your meat pour off the drippings; if too much fat pour part of it into a jar kept for that purpose; it will be found good for frying; mix one tablespoonful of flour with a little water; rub it smooth; add to the drippings left in the pan; as it browns pour boiling water on, adding more water as it thickens, stirring all the time. If lumpy, strain the gravy. Mutton drippings must never be used for cooking. Gravies for poultry are made the same as for roasting meats.

DRAWN BUTTER.

Rub two teaspoonfuls of flour into a quarter of a pound of butter; add five tablespoonfuls of cold water; set it into boiling water and let it melt and heat until it begins to simmer. Be careful not to have the flour in lumps; if it is to be used for fish put in chopped eggs and nasturtions or capers. If used with boiled fowl, put in oysters while it is simmering; let them heat through.

ANOTHER WAY OF PREPARING DRAWN BUTTER.

Make three teaspoonfuls of flour into a thin batter; stir it into a teacup of boiling water in a saucepan; let it boil five minutes; then take it off and cut up a quarter of a pound of butter into pieces and put in and keep hot until it is melted. This is the easiest way; if it is for very rich cooking add more butter.

NICE FOR GRAVY OR SOUP.

Take butter size of an egg; add a tablespoonful of sugar; put it in a skillet; stir it until a dark brown; then dredge in flour and use it to darken gravy or soup.

GRAVIES AND SAUCES.

WINE SAUCE FOR MUTTON OR VENISON.

Take half a pint of the liquor in which the meat was cooked; when boiling, put in pepper, salt, currant jelly and wine to your taste; add a teaspoonful of scorched flour mixed with a little water.

OYSTER SAUCE.

Take a pint of oyster juice, add a little salt and pepper, a stick of mace, boil it five minutes, then add two teaspoonfuls of flour, wet up in half a teacup of milk; let this boil two minutes, then put in the oysters, and a bit of butter size of an egg; in two minutes take them up.

CELERY SAUCE FOR BOILED FOWLS.

Take four or five celery heads, cut up all but the green tops into small pieces; boil it in half a pint of water till tender. Mix two teaspoonfuls of flour with a little milk, and put in a saltspoonful of salt, butter size of an egg; when it boils take it up.

MINT SAUCE FOR ROAST LAMB.

Two tablespoonfuls of green mint, one tablespoonful of pounded sugar, and a quarter of a pint of vinegar. Pick and wash the green mint very clean; chop it fine; mix the sugar and vinegar in a sauce tureen; put in the mint; let it stand.

VENISON GRAVY.

Boil the rough pieces of venison with a little mutton, beef, or any other kind of meat, nearly all one day; then let it rest quietly over night, taking off the fat in the morning; then thicken it with scorched flour; add spices and sugar to taste, with as much wine as you please.

MRS. S. S. BAILEY, Boston.

POULTRY.

All poultry should be carefully picked, and hair singed off by holding the bird over a lighted piece of paper. Take care in removing that the gall bag and the gut joining the gizzard are not broken. Open the gizzard, first take out the contents, and detach the gall bladder from the liver. If poultry is brought from market frozen, do not hasten to thaw it out before it is wanted for use; till then, put it in a cold place and let it remain frozen. When you thaw it use only cold water. Any frozen poultry or meat thawed in warm water will most certainly spoil. Food of any kind which has been frozen requires a much longer time to cook.

ROAST TURKEY.

Take a fine large turkey, if too fat take part of it out, singe it carefully; see that the inside and craw are all removed, saving the giblets (neck, heart gizzard and liver) for the gravy. After it is thoroughly cleaned, wash the inside well, wipe it dry, make a dressing of stale bread crumbs, a little salt and pepper, some sweet herbs if liked; add to this a hard boiled egg chopped fine. It may all be moistened with a little water or lemon juice, and some good white wine. Stuff the turkey well with the dressing, both the neck and the body, then sew it up. Cut up the giblets; put them into a small saucepan with very little water; stew them while the turkey is roasting; add a piece of fresh butter dredged with flour; when done take out the pieces of neck, retaining those of the heart, liver and gizzard; stir into the gravy after it comes from the fire, the yolk of a beaten egg; skim the gravy in the dripping pan; add it to the gravy made of the giblets.

A roast turkey may be stuffed with oysters, or with chestnuts boiled, peeled and mashed with butter. If with chestnuts, thicken the gravy with whole boiled chestnuts. If with oysters, send oyster sauce to table with the turkey. If chestnuts cannot be obtained, any roasted poultry is good stuffed with well-boiled sweet potatoes mashed with plenty of butter or meat drippings.

BOILED TURKEY.

Prepare and stuff the turkey as for roasting; a nice dressing is made by chopping half a pint of oysters and mixing them with bread crumbs, butter, pepper and salt, thyme or sweet marjoram; wet with milk or water; sew up the turkey in a thin cloth, first dredging the inside with flour; put it in to boil in cold water with a spoonful of salt in it; skim it while boiling; if very large will take from two to three hours. Serve with oyster sauce made by adding to a cupful of the liquor the turkey was boiled in the same quantity of milk and eight oysters chopped fine; season with minced parsley; stir in a spoonful of rice or wheat flour wet with cold milk, and a tablespoonful of butter. Boil up once and pour into a tureen.

ROAST GOOSE.

A goose for roasting should be young, tender and fat; so tender that the skin can be easily torn by a pin; if old, no cooking can make it eatable. Geese are not good for boiling or in a pie. In preparing a goose for cooking, save the giblets for the gravy; after the goose has been drawn, singed well, wiped inside and out, make a quantity of dressing; for this purpose parboil two good sized onions and a bunch of green sage; chop both the sage and onions, seasoning them with a saltspoon of salt, half as much black pepper, and still less cayenne; add a hard boiled egg finely minced. If your goose is large take two chopped eggs. To make the stuffing very mild, add a handful of grated bread crumbs, or two or three juicy chopped apples; fill the body and craw with the dressing; secure it with a needle and thread from falling out; set the goose in a baking pan with a little water; keep it well basted; it must be thoroughly done all through. It will take from an hour and a half to two hours to roast, according to its size. The gravy for roast goose may be made the same as for roast turkey.

ROAST PHEASANTS, PARTRIDGES, ETC.

See that your birds are thoroughly cleaned; chop some fine raw oysters, omitting the hard part; mix with salt and nutmeg; add the beaten yolk of an egg to bind the other ingredients; cut some very thin slices of pickled pork and cover the birds with them; then wrap them closely in sheets of white paper well buttered; put them in a baking pan and roast by a quick fire. Send them to the table with oyster sauce. Pies may be made of any of these birds the same as a pigeon pie.

ROAST DUCK.

Take a pair of fine fat ducks; put them for a few minutes into boiling water to loosen the skin, which must be peeled entirely off in order to be nice and tender; wash them thoroughly inside, wipe the outside all over with a dry cloth, fill the body and craw with a seasoning of sage and onions, as for a goose. Roast them well; baste them all the time; make a gravy mixed with what has been made of the necks, livers, hearts and gizzards stewed in a small saucepan, with a lump of butter dredged with flour; skim the fat off; pour over the ducks. The fishy taste wild ducks have is entirely destroyed by having an onion dressing.

BOILED DUCK.

Make a paste of half a pound of butter to a pound of flour; put into the inside a little salt and pepper, one or two sage leaves and a little onion finely chopped; inclose the duck in the paste with a little jellied gravy. Boil it in a cloth; serve with brown gravy.

POULTRY.

CHICKENS.

Whether for boiling or roasting should be prepared and have a dressing made the same as for turkeys. Six spoonfuls of rice boiled with the chickens will make them look white. If the water is cold when put in, they will be less liable to break; they are improved by boiling a little salt pork with them. Chickens broiled should be split down the back; inwards taken out and then thoroughly washed; broil very slowly, placing the bony side down on the gridiron; as soon as nicely brown turn it on the other side. Chickens and game of all kinds may be prepared the same as for broiling by putting them in a baking pan; dredge with flour, season with salt and pepper, and water enough to keep from burning; baste frequently.

CHICKEN PIE.

Cut up and parboil a pair of chickens; season with pepper, salt and nutmeg; prepare your dough same as for pie crust; line the sides of the dish with the dough; put an inverted teacup in the middle of the dish; fill round it a layer of chicken, a layer of raw potatoes cut very thin, with salt and pepper and a few thin slices of pickled pork; add as much of the liquor the chickens were boiled in as will fill the dish. Then cover the whole with a lid of paste. Important to make a cross slit in the top to let the steam escape; bake the pie about an hour or more.

QUAIL PIE.

Take a tender beefsteak, cut it into pieces, say one or two pounds, and lay it raw upon the under crust in the bottom of the dish, cover the beef with salt and pepper and small pieces of onions shred fine; put a small dust of black pepper inside of each quail, and put seven or eight into a pie on the beefsteak, then put a very small quantity of water into the dish, put on a top crust and bake. The gravy is to be put in through the rose on the top of the crust with a small funnel, so as not to spill over the crust. The gravy is to be made the day previous, if possible, as follows: take a piece of veal or beef, one blade of mace, two cloves and four or five allspice; stew them together in a saucepan till the flavor of the spice is out; the gravy should be a little rich with the fat, on account of the birds being dry; strain the gravy through a sieve and pour it into the pie, hot as you can, with the funnel as before named. Chicken pie the same. Cut up the back, head, neck and gizzard for the gravy.   MRS. SAM'L TREAT.

STEWED CHICKEN WITH OYSTERS.

Season and stew a chicken in a quart of water until very tender, but not to fall from the bones; take it out on a hot dish and keep it warm; then put into the liquor in which it was stewed, a lump of butter the size of an egg; mix a little flour and water, smooth, and make thick gravy; season well with pepper and salt and let it come to a boil; have ready a quart of oysters picked over, and put them in without any of the liquor; stir them around, and as soon as they are cooked pour all over the chicken.   MRS. J. F. E.

FRIED CHICKEN.

After cleaning the chicken, cut and quarter; put some lard in a skillet and fry the pieces; when done take the pieces out; rub into the lard, until perfectly smooth, a tablespoonful of flour, with salt and pepper to season; then add a cupful of milk or cream; let all come to a boil; then pour over the fried chicken.

FRIED CHICKEN.

Beat two eggs, to which add a little milk; pepper and salt your chicken, dip it in your eggs and milk, and then in grated cracker; fry in butter until brown.   MRS. DAVIS.

FRICASSEED CHICKEN.

The chickens should be washed, jointed; take out the inwards; place them in a stew pan and sprinkle with salt and pepper, add three or four slices of pork, cover with water and stew until tender; on taking them up mix a little flour and water, a piece of butter size of a hen's egg, pour it into the liquor the chickens were stewed in; a little mace, nutmeg or sweet herbs may be added if liked; after putting all the ingredients together let it simmer, but do not let it boil; watch it carefully. Half a pint of boiling cream, a large teaspoonful arrow root and the beaten yolks of two eggs mixed with more cream may also be added.

TO COOK AN OLD CHICKEN.

Wash carefully and fill with buttered bread crumbs, seasoned with pepper, salt and thyme; put in a pot with a tight fitting cover with about a pint of water; turn often and cook two hours or until tender.

CHICKEN STUFFED WITH OYSTERS.

Take a young chicken, stuff it with raw oysters and a little salt; put in a stone jar tightly covered; set that in a pot of cold water; if a tender chicken it will boil in half hour; when done take the chicken out, put it on a platter, then take the liquor that is left in the jar, pour it in a stew pan, mix two tablespoonfuls of flour, a very little cayenne pepper, little salt, half teaspoonful of Worcestershire sauce in the liquor, boil a few moments, when done pour over the chicken. A very nice dish for invalids, leaving out the pepper and sauce.   Mrs. E. D. Lowe.

SMOTHERED CHICKEN.

Cut the chickens in the back; lay them flat in a dripping pan with one cup of water; let them stew in the oven until they begin to get tender; take them out and season with salt and pepper. Rub together one and one-half tablespoonfuls of flour, one tablespoonful of butter, spread all over the chicken; put back in the oven, baste well, and when tender and nicely brown take out of the dripping pan. Mix with the gravy in the pan one cup of milk thickened with a little flour, put on top of the stove and let it scald up well, and pour over the chicken; parsley chopped fine is a nice addition to the gravy.   MAGGIE FANNING.

JELLIED CHICKEN.

Take one large chicken, or two small ones; boil them in a quart of water till tender; cut off the meat, put the skin and bones back into the liquor and boil this down to a pint of jelly (about three quarters of an hour). Chop up the meat of the chicken and pound it fine; add to it a teaspoonful of powdered mustard, one of salt, one of butter, a little pepper and half a teacupful of the liquid jelly, from which you must strain the bones and skin; the remainder of the liquid jelly pour into the bottom of the mould and let it cool; put the pounded chicken in a saucepan and warm it so that all the ingredients may be thoroughly mixed; then let it cool and spread it on top of the jelly in the mould; set the mould in a cool place; when wanted to serve set the mould for an instant in warm water and turn out like blanc mange.

MRS. H. N. DAVIS.

BONED CHICKEN.

Take a chicken, parboil it, then slit down the back, taking out the back-bone and ribs; stuff with force meat, lard the breast, making two rows down on each side; bake in the oven, basting well, and serve with tomato sauce on the dish.

FORCE MEAT.—Finely chopped lamb or tongue seasoned with small pieces of pork, summer savory, peper, salt and *plenty* of lemon.   MRS. J. G. CHAPMAN.

SNIPE AND WOODCOCKS.

Pick them immediately; wipe them very clean outside, drawing out the one gut from the inside, leaving the heart, liver, etc., in. Truss them with the legs close to the body, and the feet pressing upon the thighs; skin the head and neck, and bring the beak round under the wing. After the birds are picked and trussed, put a thin layer of bacon over them, and tie it on; toast and butter a slice of bread, and put it under them for the trail to drop on. Baste them continually with butter, and roast them; if large, will take twenty-five minutes. Take up the toast, cut it in quarters, put it in a dish, and pour some gravy and butter over it. Take up the birds, put them on it with the bills outwards. Serve with plain butter sauce.

STUFFED QUAILS.

After the birds have been dressed and washed in cold water, tie across the breast of each a thin slice of bacon. Stuff each bird with the following stuffing, and bake in a dripping pan, basting them thoroughly. Stuffing: Slice quite fine three bunches of celery; cut in small pieces one can of prepared mushrooms, and half a can of tomatoes. Mix them with enough bread crumbs to make the stuffing easy to handle and fill each bird as full as possible.

Mrs. J. G. Chapman.

SMALL BIRDS BROILED.

After being dressed, split them down the the back; spread them flat and broil them very gently over a bright fire of coals; butter, salt and pepper them, and serve quickly.

Mrs. Lewis E. Kline.

POTTED PIGEONS.

Take four or five slices of pork, and cut into small bits, and fry out till it is crispy. Stir the pork all the time, then turn it into the bottom of the kettle. Clean the pigeons nicely. Clean the hearts, livers and gizzards, and put them aside in a bowl of cold water. Then make a nice dressing of pork, bread, sage and pepper; have it hard enough to roll into balls; stuff the pigeons and lay them on their backs in a kettle; cover them with cold water; season with pepper and salt. If tender they will cook in an hour and a half; if old, they will take two and a half or more. Fifteen or twenty minutes before you take them off, take four spoonfuls of flour, mixed with enough water to get out the lumps, and put in the kettle. The water will probably have boiled away, so add enough boiling water to cover them, and let them have one good boil up. Put the inwards in to boil when you do the pigeons. Be sure to keep a tea-kettle of boiling water handy, in order to replenish. Turn the kettle round frequently, that the pigeons may not burn. MRS. J. T. DAVIS.

VEAL OR POULTRY CAKE.

Chop cold veal or chicken very fine; mix two cups of the meat with one cup of bread crumbs that have soaked in milk; add half a cup of cream, two tablespoons of melted butter, one egg well beaten, pepper and salt and a little nutmeg; bake in a deep dish, and eat cold, cut in slices.

MRS. KRUM.

CHICKEN CHEESE.

Two chickens boiled tender; chop them but not too fine; season with salt and pepper; boil three or four eggs and slice them; line moulds or dishes with these; pour in the chicken and add the liquor they boiled in; when cold, slice for lunch or tea. MRS. D. YOUNG.

CHICKEN CHEESE.

Boil an old chicken until most to pieces; take out all the bones, and chop the meat fine; season well and pour in enough of the broth to make moist; press into moulds to get cold, slice them. MISS E. TUCKER.

CHICKEN SAUTE A LA MANGE.

Cut a raw chicken into ten parts; put sweet oil in sauce pan; fry both sides brown; add garlic chopped with parsley to suit taste; dredge with flour and fill with water or beef stock; cover close and stew in oven until done; add mushrooms or truffles; fry eggs on both sides and serve with chicken. REVERE HOUSE.

CHICKEN OR VEAL CROQUETTES.

Chop roast or boiled chicken or veal as fine as mince meat; pound it with a potato masher; take sauce of milk or cream thickened with flour and butter (similar to drawn butter), half an onion chopped fine; scald a piece of celery in the sauce (and then remove it); season with pepper and salt; mix together very soft; make into the form of sausages; put them on ice for several hours; when wanted for serving, dip them in beaten eggs and bread crumbs and fry in lard until brown. A little parsley improves them.

CHICKEN CROQUETTES.

Boil two chickens, mince fine; two small onions, mince fine; one bunch of parsley minced fine; salt and cayenne pepper to taste; rind of one lemon, minced fine; mix all together with three-fourths cup of cream; roll in bread crumbs; dip in eggs; roll in cracker meal, and fry brown.

MRS. CORNELIA BEER.

CROQUETTE OF FOWL.

Mince the fowl, removing all skin and bone; fry three or four small onions in one ounce of butter; add the chopped fowl; dredge in one teaspoonful of flour; add pepper, salt, pounded mace and one-half teaspoonful fine sugar; sufficient soup stock to moisten it; stir also in it the yolks of two well beaten eggs, and set it by to cool; then make the mixture up into balls; egg and bread crumb them, and fry a nice brown.

MRS. G. LEIGHTON.

CROQUETTES.

Cut roast veal, or the white part of roast turkey or chicken, into small dice. Stir together a tablespoonful of flour and butter; melt and thin it with a little chicken broth and cream; let it boil till thick; season with a little nutmeg, pepper, salt and lemon peel. Put in the minced meat and let it simmer for ten or fifteen minutes; put the mixture on a platter to cool; then form into balls and roll them twice in egg and bread crumbs. Fry in boiling lard, in a deep kettle. MRS. J. M. KRUM.

CHICKEN CROQUETTES.

Take the remnants of chicken or turkey, chop fine, add pepper, salt and a little spice; mix with this one-quarter as much bread crumbs as you have meat; make into pointed balls and add two tablespoons of melted butter; roll these in beaten egg and rolled cracker, and fry in butter or lard; serve dry and hot; garnish with parsley if desired.

CROQUETTES.

One large chicken boiled until very soft; just before done drop two sets calves' brains, tied up in thin muslin cloth, in to boil; when they are all thoroughly boiled, chopped very fine, add one cup beef suet chopped fine, season well with salt, pepper, parsley, nutmeg, and the juice of one lemon; if stiff add a little cream; make as soft as you can roll, and make any shape you choose; dip in yolk of egg, then rolled cracker, and fry in plenty of boiling lard like an oyster.

MRS. HUGH CAMPBELL.

SALADS.

FOR CHICKEN OR LOBSTER.

Use either celery or lettuce, about as much as you have meat; chop fine or coarse to taste; salt well. For dressing for one or two chickens, take yolks of two raw and two hard boiled eggs, one tablespoonful dry mustard and stirring in one direction; slowly add one-third of a half pint bottle of olive oil, juice of one lemon, then more oil until two-thirds of the bottle is used; add a little vinegar and salt; mix this slowly, stirring one way well; it will get thick and rich as cream. Mix dressing and chicken just before using; by keeping covered the dressing will keep several hours. If turkey is preferred to chicken use only the breast; but if chicken, all the meat can be used; skin it, of course; instead of chopping, some tear the meat into shreds; if chopped, do not mince too fine. MISS R. ROBERTS.

SALAD DRESSING.

Yolks of two eggs boiled hard and mashed very fine; break in two raw eggs well beaten, one tablespoonful of mustard, one of sugar, a little salt, one cup of olive oil; put in the oil by the teaspoonful, beating hard all the time; one cup of cream, half a cup of vinegar, put in the last thing.
MRS. W. H. PULSIFER.

CHICKEN SALAD.

Boil two nice chickens; when cold remove all the meat and chop rather fine; wash and separate two large heads of celery; cut the tender part into pieces about an inch long, and chop the remainder with the chicken; take the yolks of eight hard boiled eggs and mash them to a paste with the back

of a spoon; add one small teaspoonful of fine salt, the same of cayenne pepper, four tablespoonfuls made mustard, a wineglass and a half of good vinegar, same quantity of best table oil; then add the yolk of one raw egg well beaten; mix all together thoroughly until quite smooth. Pour it on the chicken and celery and mix all together with a silver fork.
MRS. FRANK FILLEY.

DRESSING FOR CHICKEN SALAD.

Yolks of two eggs beaten very light, two teaspoonfuls mustard, one teaspoonful sugar, one teaspoonful salt; beat together until thick; pour gradually and beat into it one pint of olive oil; when thick, thin with vinegar, and add at the last a little cream.
MRS. R. H. MORTON.

POTATO SALAD

Slice or cut in small pieces cold boiled potatoes; rub on a bowl an onion to get just a slight flavor of the onion; then mix a dressing of two yolks of raw eggs rubbed smooth, two mustardspoons of mustard, two saltspoons of salt, and pepper; then add four tablespoons of best salad oil very gradually, two tablespoons of sharp vinegar. Chopped parsley and chopped celery stalks are a great addition. It is better to have the dressing poured over the salad two or three hours before using.
MRS. E. F. RICHARDS.

SALAD DRESSING.

Yolk of one egg (raw); one teaspoon each of salt, sugar and dry mustard, a very little cayenne pepper, two tablespoonfuls of vinegar, one quarter of a large bottle of oil. Put the ingredients, except the oil and vinegar, in a soup plate, mix very smooth with a salad fork; then add the oil and vinegar alternately, very little at a time, stirring constantly till thick and smooth. Set in a cool place till needed.
MISS KRUM.

SALAD DRESSING.

The yolks of four eggs (raw); two-thirds cup of olive oil; one tablespoonful mixed mustard; one teaspoonful salt; one teaspoonful sugar; beat these together, adding the oil very slowly. When well mixed, add two-thirds cup of vinegar; set it on the stove, or over boiling water, to thicken; when cool add the whites, which must be beaten to a foam; mix part with the salad, leaving some to pour over the top; garnish with hard boiled eggs sliced.

Mrs. L. B. M., Boston.

SALAD DRESSING.

One hard boiled egg, mix one tablespoonful of vinegar, if weak, two; six tablespoonfuls of oil, one teaspoonful of mixed mustard, one of salt and pepper, one egg not cooked.

Mrs. Lanes.

MR. T.'S LETTUCE DRESSING.

Take four hard boiled eggs, rub the yolks till fine, and mix with tablespoon of mustard wet with vinegar; two teaspoons of powdered sugar, two teaspoons of butter, a little salt; sometimes sweet oil is used instead of butter. Cut the lettuce fine, and pour the dressing over it. Dress the top with the whites of eggs cut in rings.

LETTUCE SALAD.

The yolk of an egg rubbed smooth, one spoon of made mustard, saltspoon of salt, pepper; then add two tablespoons of olive oil, gradually; one tablespoon of sharp vinegar.

Mrs. J. T. Davis.

SLAW DRESSING.

Take a spoonful of butter, rub into it a little flour; add one tablespoonful of dry mustard, one teaspoonful of black pepper, one teaspoonful of salt, one teaspoonful of brown sugar, rub together; pour over it a little hot water to melt the butter; add the yolks of two eggs beaten light, then add one-half pint of cream, or more. Set it on the stove until ready to boil, stirring it all the time; do not let it boil, or it will curdle; set it on the ice until you wish to use it, then add vinegar to the taste. Should be made early in the morning or the day before, to have it cold.

MRS. CORNELIUS BEER.

COLD SLAW.

Two eggs beaten light, one-half cup of cream, a piece of butter size of as an egg; some made mustard, a little salt and cayenne pepper and strong vinegar; give it a boil up and scald the cut cabbage in it. MISS EMILY TUCKER.

SLAW DRESSING.

Two eggs beaten light, one tablespoon of mustard, one teaspoon of pepper, one of salt, one tablespoon of sugar, one cup vinegar, one of milk or cream; put this in last and stir every few minutes over a fire till it thickens.

MRS. TREAT.

HOLLAND HERRING SALAD.

Two dozen Holland herring soaked over night and skinned; allspice, pepper and mustard, sliced onion, tablespoonful of olive oil, handful of bay leaves, three lemons sliced; add the melts; vinegar to taste, pour all over the herring.

MRS. JOHN LADY.

CURRY POWDER.

Mix an ounce of ginger, one of mustard and one of pepper, three of coriander seed, the same quantity of turmeric, quarter of an ounce of cayenne pepper, half an ounce of cardamoms, the same of cummin seed and cinnamon; pound the whole fine, and keep in a bottle tightly corked.

TO MIX MUSTARD.

To one-half cup of mustard take one teaspoonful of sugar, one saltspoon of salt; mix it smooth with a very little cold vinegar, then thin it with scalding hot vinegar.

MRS. O. D. FILLEY.

HORSERADISH SAUCE.

TO SERVE WITH ROAST BEEF.

Four tablespoons grated horseradish, one teaspoon sugar, one teaspoon salt, half teaspoon pepper, two teaspoons made mustard, vinegar; mix the horseradish well with the sugar, salt, pepper and mustard; moisten it with sufficient vinegar to give it consistency of cream; serve in a tureen. Three or four tablespoons of cream added very much improves it. Serve cold with cold meats, or heat (not boil) for hot roast beef.   Mrs. Avery Plummer, Boston.

SAUCE HOLLANDAISE A LA MAISON DOREE.

Two tablespoonfuls of flour carefully mixed with one tumblerful of cold water, place over the fire, and when cooked, add pepper and salt, and a little lemmon juice, also the yolks of two eggs; then draw from the fire and add half a pound of butter, *stirring all the time.*
  Mr. J. B. G——, Paris.

SAUCE BLANCHE.

One pint of cream, one quarter of a pound of butter, one tablespoonful of flour, not heaping, pinch of salt; mix flour and butter well together, boil your cream; as soon as boiled pour part on the butter and flour; when well mixed add it to the rest of the boiling cream; serve immediately.
  Mrs. E. D. Lowe.

VEGETABLES.

STEAM POTATOES.

Peel and slice very thin the raw potatoes; lay them in cold water for a few moments; have in your skillet either a spoonful of butter or lard; put your potatoes in, season with pepper and salt, stirring them frequently to keep from burning; keep them tightly covered.   MRS. GLOVER.

TO BOIL NEW POTATOES.

Scrape the skins from new potatoes and lay them in cold water for an hour or two; put them into a saucepan and cover them with water; cover them and boil for half an hour; try one, if quite done drain the water off; let them stand for a couple of minutes; make a sauce of hot milk thickened with flour and seasoned with butter, salt and pepper; pour over the potatoes and serve hot.

MASHED POTATOES.

Pare the potatoes; put them into a saucepan with sufficient cold water to cover them; let them boil gently until tender; take them up the moment they are soft through, which can be ascertained by thrusting a fork in them; drain away the water; put the saucepan by the side of the fire with the lid partially uncovered and let the potatoes get thoroughly dry, then mash them, take a large fork and beat them very light, adding hot milk with melted butter in it, and salt to taste. Serve hot.   MRS. O. D. FILLEY.

FRIED POTATOES.

Peel and cut the potatoes in thin slices as nearly the same size as possible; make some dripping or butter quite hot in a frying pan; put in the potatoes and fry on both sides to a nice brown; when they are crisp and done take them up; place them on a cloth before the fire to drain the grease from them, and serve very hot after sprinkling with salt. These are delicious served as a breakfast dish. The remains of cold potatoes may be sliced and fried by the above recipe, but the slices must be cut a little thicker.

SARATOGA POTATOES.

Slice the potatoes very thin on a potato cutter; lay them in cold water for an hour, then drain and spread them on a dry towel; wipe each piece with a soft dry cloth and fry a few at a time in boiling lard, in a deep kettle. Take them up with a skimmer when browned lightly, and sprinkle a little fine salt over them. MRS. J. M. KRUM.

TO BROIL POTATOES.

After broiling a steak, take some cold boiled potatoes, cut lengthwise, a quarter of an inch thick, dip each piece in flour and lay them on a gridiron over a clear fire. When both sides are nicely browned, put them on a hot dish, with a piece of butter over them, and a little pepper and salt. Serve them up hot. MRS. E. F. RICHARDS.

POTATOES A LA CREME.

Put into a saucepan three tablespoonfuls of butter, a small handful of parsley, chopped small, salt and pepper to taste; stir up well until hot; add a small teacupful of cream or rich milk; thicken with a teaspoonful of flour, and stir until it boils; chop some cold boiled potatoes, put into the mixture and boil up once before serving.

MRS. J. T. DAVIS.

POTATO SCOLLOPS.

Boil and beat the potatoes with a little cream or milk, a large piece of butter, salt and pepper to taste; butter some scallop shells or patty pans, fill with the mixture and brown in an oven; when a pattern has been stamped on each, glaze while hot with butter, and serve in the shells on a napkin. Grated cheese may be strewed on top.

POTATO CROQUETTES.

Twelve potatoes boiled, mashed and pressed through a cullender; pepper, salt and a little onion, a little parsley chopped fine, and a scant tablespoon of flour, piece of butter the size of a hazel nut, yolks of two eggs; dip the croquettes in whites of the eggs; roll in powdered bread, and fry in hot lard.   Mrs. D. Young.

POTATO RICE.

Choose ten large potatoes; boil until tender, and mash; press them through a large cullender on to a hot dish before the fire; shake the cullender lightly every other minute to cause the potatoes to fall off in short grains like rice; serve very hot. This will be found a nice accompaniment to a sausage supper.   Miss Roberts.

TO BROWN POTATOES UNDER MEAT.

Boil some large mealy potatoes, take off the skin carefully, and about an hour before the meat is cooked, put them into the dripping pan, having well dredged them with flour before; drain them from any grease, and serve them hot.
                                                  Mrs. Glover.

ROAST SWEET POTATOES.

Select those of uniform size, wash, wipe and roast until mellow throughout; serve in their jackets. Sweet as well as Irish potatoes are very nice roasted in hot ashes.

BOILED SWEET POTATOES.

Put into cold water without salt; boil until a fork will easily pierce the largest; turn off the water and lay them in the oven to dry for five minutes; peel before sending to table. Or parboil and then roast until done.

FRIED SWEET POTATOES.

Boil until nearly done; skin and cut lengthwise into slices a quarter of an inch thick; fry in sweet dripping or butter.

BAKED TOMATOES.

Fill a deep dish with whole tomatoes skinned; sprinkle with bread crumbs, one tablespoonful of sugar, same of butter, salt and pepper to taste. Tomatoes may be sliced and cooked in the same way.

STUFFED BAKED TOMATOES.

Bake the tomatoes whole; then scoop out a small hole at the top and fill with fried bread crumbs and onions, or bread crumbs with butter, sugar, salt and pepper; then brown the tomatoes in an oven, and take care that the skin does not break.

FRIED TOMATOES.

Wash them, cut in slices; make a batter of flour, water and egg, and season with pepper and salt; dip each piece in the batter; have ready some melted butter in a pan; put them in it, and fry slowly till nicely brown.

Miss E. L. Glover.

STEWED TOMATOES.

Slice the tomatoes into a lined saucepan; season them with pepper and salt, and place small pieces of butter on them; cover the lid down closely, and stew from twenty to twenty-five minutes, or until the tomatoes are perfectly tender. Bread crumbs may be added if desired to thicken; a minced onion—a small one—improves the flavor. Another variety is, to add a quarter as much green corn as tomatoes, into the saucepan when first put on the fire.

BOILED GREEN CORN.

Take young sugar corn; clean by stripping off the outer leaves; turn back the innermost covering, pick off the silk and recover the ear with the husk that grew nearest it; tie at the top; put in boiling salted water, and cook fast about half an hour; send to the table wrapped in a napkin.

SUCCOTASH.

Cut from the cob, not too closely, young sugar corn; scraping off with a knife what is left on the cob. Take a third more corn than beans, when the former has been cut from the cob, and the latter shelled; put the beans into boiling water enough to cover them, and cook half an hour before the corn is put on, which should be boiled half an hour; put both together; add a cup of rich milk or cream, a large piece of butter, salt and pepper to taste; cook slowly for half an hour; watch closely to prevent burning.

MARY COLBURT.

SUCCOTASH.

One quart of Lima beans put on in two quarts of cold water; while boiling cut the corn from a dozen ears, and boil the cobs for a few minutes with the beans; when the beans are done, stir the corn with the beans, and add one cup of cream, one tablespoon of butter, one teaspoon of sugar, salt and pepper to taste; the corn should cook twenty minutes. A small piece of salt pork cooked with the beans is a great improvement.

MRS. C. B. RICHARDS.

STEWED GREEN CORN.

Cut from the cob and stew in boiling water, fifteen minutes; turn off most of the water; cover with cold milk, and stew until tender, adding a large lump of butter, cut in small pieces, rolled in flour; season with salt and pepper to taste.

CORN CAKES OR MOCK OYSTERS.

One pint of grated green corn, three tablespoons of milk, one-half cup of melted butter, one teaspoon of salt, one-half of pepper, one egg; bake on a griddle; flour to stiffen.

LIMA BEANS.

Boil about an hour; pour the water off; season with salt, pepper and butter; send to the table hot.

Dried Lima beans must be soaked over night, and boiled two hours, or until they are soft, and should have some um added to the dressing.

MACARONI.

One-half pound of macaroni boiled in a quart of milk and water for one hour, teaspoonful of salt put in a dish, and cover the top with grated cheese; bake for three-quarters of an hour.

ITALIAN MACARONI.

Take three pints of beef soup; clean and put into it one pound of macaroni; add a little salt and boil fifteen minutes. Then take up the macaroni, which should have absorbed most of the soup; put it on a flat dish, sprinkle grated cheese over it thickly and pour over it all plentifully a sauce made of tomatoes well boiled, strained and seasoned with salt and pepper. This is excellent. MRS. H. MCKITTRICK.

MACARONI A LA CREME.

Boil ten minutes in salted boiling water; drain; add a cup of milk; stew until tender; heat to boiling in another saucepan a cup of milk thickened with a teaspoonful of flour, a tablespoonful of butter and a beaten egg. When this thickens pour over the macaroni after it is dished. This may be eaten with butter, sugar and nutmeg, or if served with meat, grate cheese thickly over it.

BOILED HOMINY.

Large hominy, soak over night in cold water; next day put it into a pot with at least two quarts of water to a quart of hominy and boil slowly three or more hours until it is soft; drain in a cullender and stir in butter, pepper and salt. Small hominy may be cooked in the same way, stirring almost constantly at the last. It should be thick as mush and eaten with sugar, cream and nutmeg.

FRIED HOMINY.

Cut in slices cold boiled hominy and fry in hot lard or drippings, or moisten with milk; add melted butter; bind with a beaten egg; form into round cakes; dredge with flour and fry a light brown.

HOMINY CROQUETTES.

Take one cupful of cold boiled hominy; add one cup of sweet milk, one egg well beaten, two tablespoonfuls of butter, a teaspoonful of white sugar; mix well; roll into oval balls with floured hands; dip in beaten egg, then cracker crumbs, and fry in hot lard.

BAKED HOMINY.

Beat three eggs very light, yolks and whites separately; work the yolks first into a cupful of cold boiled hominy, alternately with a heaping teaspoonful of butter; when thoroughly mixed put in a teaspoonful of white sugar, a little salt and go on beating until smooth, while you soften the butter gradually with two cups of milk. Stir in the whites and bake in a buttered pudding dish until light, firm and brown a delicate color.

MASHED CARROTS.

Wash, scrape and lay in cold water awhile; boil tender in hot water, slightly salted; drain, mash smoothly, adding butter, salt and pepper; a little cream will improve them; mould and stamp a figure upon them.

BOILED CARROTS.

Wash and scrape well, and lay in cold water half an hour; if large, split them; boil until tender; butter well and serve hot.

CARROTS A LA FLAMADE.

Boil six or eight good sized carrots until tender; cut them into stars or dice; then stew them with five small onions, a sprig of chopped parsley, a little pepper and salt, three-quarters of a pint of good gravy, or a little melted butter; serve very hot.

FRIED EGG PLANT.

Slice the egg plant in round slices; pare carefully; lay in salt and water for an hour or more; wipe the slices dry, dip in beaten eggs, then in bread or cracker crumbs, and fry them brown in hot lard, or lard and butter in equal quantities; drain well and serve hot.

BAKED EGG PLANT.

Cut the egg plant lengthwise; take out all of the insides, leaving the skin thick enough to keep the shape; chop up the inside in a wooden bowl, with half a teacupful of bread crumbs, one tablespoonful of butter, salt and pepper to taste; after mixing well, put it into the skins, lay them in a pan side by side, with a little water; bake about three-quarters of an hour.   MRS. WM. G. ELIOT.

EGG PLANT.

Pare and slice one large egg plant, and let it soak for half an hour in salt and water; then boil until soft enough to mash; yolk of one egg, one cup of milk, and flour enough to make a thin batter; stir in the egg plant and fry like fritters in boiling lard.

TO BOIL RICE.

Wash one teacupful of rice three times in boiling water; put in a quart of boiling water, and boil fast twenty minutes; strain through a cullender; shake the steam out and serve immediately.   MRS. E. F. RICHARDS.

STEWED ONIONS.

Skin and lay in cold water half an hour or more; put into a saucepan with hot water enough to cover them; when half done, throw off all the water, except a small teacupful; add a like quantity of milk, a large spoonful of butter, with pepper and salt to taste; stew gently until tender, and turn into a deep dish. If the onions are large, boil in three waters, reserving a little of the third to mix with the milk. The disagreeable odor left by the onions upon the breath may be removed by chewing and swallowing a few grains of roasted coffee.

BAKED SPANISH ONIONS.

Put the onions, with their skins on, into a saucepan of boiling water, slightly salted, and let them boil quickly for an hour; then take them out, wipe them thoroughly, wrap each one in a piece of paper separately, and bake them in a moderate oven for two hours or longer, should the onions be very large. They may be served in their skins and eaten with a seasoning of butter, pepper and salt; or they may be peeled, put into a deep dish, and browned slightly, basting with butter freely; serve in a vegetable dish, and pour over the melted butter when you have sprinkled with pepper.

CELERY.

Cut off the roots, wash and scrape the stalks, cut off the green leaves; if the celery is large, divide it lengthwise into quarters, and curl the tops; put in cold water until sent to the table.

CELERY A LA CREME.

Wash the celery thoroughly; trim, boil in salt and water until tender; boil until smooth, half a pint of cream with a piece of butter rolled in flour, a little salt and grated nutmeg; dish the celery, pour over the sauce, and serve hot.

BOILED SPINACH.

Pick the spinach very clean; wash in several waters until clean; put in cold water for half an hour; then put in boiling water, with a little salt in it, and boil until tender; drain through a cullender; chop fine; then put it into a saucepan, with a piece of butter the size of an egg, and a little pepper. Stew over the fire until very hot, and put into a dish; garnish with poached eggs at the top, or sliced hard boiled eggs.

SPINACH A LA CREME.

Boil until tender; chop very fine; rub through a cullender; season with pepper, salt, and a little grated nutmeg. Put in a saucepan; stir over the fire until warm; pour in

VEGETABLES.

three tablespoonfuls of cream; add a quarter of a pound of butter, and a teaspoonful of pounded sugar. Stir it over the fire for five minutes, and serve it piled high in the centre of the dish, or pressed into a form, garnished with boiled eggs.

SALSIFY, OR VEGETABLE OYSTER.

Scrape the roots thoroughly; lay in cold water half an hour. If large, split them; put in boiling water, slightly salted, and boil until tender. Turn off nearly all the water, and add a cupful of cold milk. Stew ten minutes after it begins to boil; add a lump of butter rolled in flour; pepper and salt to taste; boil up once, and serve.

FRIED SALSIFY, OR MOCK OYSTERS.

Scrape the roots and lay in cold water fifteen minutes; boil whole until tender; drain, and, when cold, mash to a smooth paste, picking out the fibres; moisten with a little milk, add a tablespoonful of butter, an egg, a cup of salsify; beat the eggs light; make into round cakes; dredge with flour, and fry brown.

BOILED PARSNIPS.

If the parsnips are young they require only to be scraped before boiling; old ones must be pared thin and split; put them into boiling salted water; boil until tender, take them up, drain them and slice lengthwise, buttering well when dished. They are generally served with boiled beef, pork, or salt cod, and also added as a garnish with boiled carrots.

FRIED PARSNIPS.

Boil until tender, then skin and cut them in lengthwise slices of a quarter of an inch in thickness. Dredge with flour, and fry in boiling butter or hot dripping, turning when one side is browned. Drain, pepper, and serve hot, with roast meat.

PARSNIPS, BOILED AND BROWNED
UNDER ROAST BEEF.

Wash and scrape, and, if large, split the parsnips. Put them into boiling salt and water, and boil quickly until tender. Take them up, drain dry, and put them in the dripping pan under roast beef; dredge over them a little pepper and salt, and brown nicely. Serve them in a separate dish, with a few as a garnish around the meat.

PARSNIPS, MASHED.

Boil and scrape, mash smooth with the back of a wooden spoon, with a few spoonfuls of cream, a large spoonful of butter, pepper and salt to taste. Heat to boiling in a saucepan, and serve.

STEWED PARSNIPS.

Pare and boil tender; cut in slices and put them into a stewpan, with half a pint of cream, a piece of butter rolled in flour, grated nutmeg and salt; shake over the fire till well mixed: dish them and garnish with parsley.

BOILED CABBAGE.

Take a head of cabbage, wash the leaves carefully, chop fine; put into a pot with cold water, boil half an hour; then pour the water off, add more hot water; let it boil another half hour, drain the cabbage, add a half cup of milk, thickened with a little flour, and a lump of butter; season with salt and pepper; let it all just come to a boil; serve hot. Cooked in this way, is almost as delicate as cauliflower.

CABBAGE WITH FORCE MEAT A LA FRANCAISE.

Take off the outer leaves of a large cabbage; scald in hot water for ten minutes; make a hole in the middle, by the side of the stalk, and fill it and between each leaf, with minced beef or mutton highly seasoned, or with some sausage force meat; bind it round neatly and stand it in a stewpan with some stock, a slice of bacon, a sprig of thyme,

VEGETABLES.

the bay leaf and two carrots; let all stew gently, and when done place the cabbage on a dish, untie the string and pour strained gravy over it. Garnish with carrots and turnips, and serve hot.

SUMMER SQUASH.

Wash, pare, quarter; take out the seeds and lay the pieces in cold water; boil until tender; drain well, pressing out all the water; mash soft and smooth, seasoning with butter, pepper and salt; serve hot. Winter squash and pumpkins are cooked in the same way.

BAKED SQUASH.

Select a good pumpkin; take out the seeds; cut in quarters; pare and slice lengthwise half an inch thick; arrange in layers, not more than two or three slices deep, in a shallow baking dish; put a very little water in the bottom; bake slowly until dry. Butter each strip on both sides when you dish, and eat hot with bread and butter for tea.

BOILED TURNIP.

Pare the turnips, and, if large, divide into quarters; put them into a saucepan of boiling salted water and boil gently until tender; then drain them dry and rub through a cullender with a wooden spoon, add a tablespoonful of cream or milk, and put into another stewpan with a large piece of butter, white pepper, and, if necessary, salt; stir over the fire until thoroughly mixed and very hot. Dish them up and serve.

TURNIPS IN WHITE SAUCE.

Peel and cut the turnips in the shape of pears or marbles; boil them in salt and water, to which has been added a little butter, until tender; then take them out; arrange on a dish; pour over a sauce made of a pint and a half of milk, boiled with an ounce and a half of rice, and one strip of lemon peel, until the rice is tender; then take out the lemon peel and pound the milk and rice together; put it back in the stewpan to warm; add mace and seasoning and give it one boil. The sauce should be of the consistency of cream.

BOILED BEETS.

Wash, boil until tender, rub off the skin, and slice; heat to boiling a large tablespoonful of melted butter, with four or five of vinegar, pepper and salt, and pour over them.

Mrs. O. D. Filley.

ASPARAGUS.

Scrape the white parts of the stem, beginning from the head; put in cold water; tie them into bundles, keeping the heads all one way, and cut the stalks evenly; put them into salted boiling water, and boil quickly until tender, with the saucepan uncovered; when the asparagus is done, dish it upon toast, which should be dipped in the water it was cooked in, and leave the white ends outwards each way, with the points meeting in the middle; serve with melted butter.

ASPARAGUS IN FRENCH ROLLS.

Cut the green part off of fifty young asparagus; wash well, boil and strain them; take half a dozen French rolls, cut a piece neatly out of the top crusts, taking care that they will fit again; pick all the crumb out of the inside, and crisp them before the fire, or fry brown in butter; then take half a pint of cream, with the yolks of four or five eggs; beat in it a little salt and nutmeg, and stir well over a slow fire until it begins to thicken; put in three parts of the asparagus, cut small; then fill the rolls with them, put on the tops; make holes in them, stick some asparagus in as if it were growing; put on a dish and serve hot.

ASPARAGUS PUDDING.

Cut up the green tender parts of the asparagus about the size of peas; put in a basin with four eggs well beaten, and one tablespoonful of finely minced ham, butter, pepper and salt; mix all well together and moisten with sufficient milk to make a thick batter; put into a pint buttered mould, tie down tightly with a floured cloth, place it in boiling water, and let it boil for two hours; turn it out of the mould on to a hot dish, and pour plain melted butter around, but not over the pudding.

BOILED CAULIFLOWER.

Choose large white cauliflowers; pick off the leaves, cut the stalk off flat at the bottom; wash well, and soak in cold water half an hour; tie in a close net of bobinet lace, to prevent its breaking; put into boiling water, salted, and cook until tender; drain and serve with plain melted butter; or a sauce may be made of half a cupful of milk, thickened with a very little rice or flour, and two tablespoons of melted butter, pepper and salt, poured over the cauliflower.

SCOLLOPED CAULIFLOWER.

Boil until tender; cut in small clusters and put in a buttered pudding dish, with the stems downward; cover the cauliflower with a cupful of bread crumbs, mixed with two tablespoons of melted butter, and three of cream or milk; bind with a beaten egg; cover the dish, and bake six minutes in a quick oven; brown in five more, and serve hot.

CAULIFLOWERS WITH PARMESAN CHEESE.

Cleanse and boil the cauliflowers; drain and dish them with the flowers upright; pour over them a cupful of clarified or melted butter; sprinkle a quarter of a pound of Parmesan cheese over the top; season with pepper, salt and nutmeg to taste; brown and serve.

BAKED BEANS.

Soak three pints beans over night; in the morning boil in fresh water until they begin to crack open. Put in a stone pot to bake with one and a half pounds of salt pork;

till up with water, in which stir two tablespoons of molasses: bake five or six hours, or over night.

Mrs. T. T. Richards.

TO COOK STRING BEANS.

A large spoonful of lard, three-fourths spoonful of flour, two yolks of eggs, two or three spoonfuls of cream or milk. Put the lard in a vessel on the fire, and when very hot mix the flour with it until quite brown: then put the beans, with enough water to cook them, in the mixture; when cooked, let them cool a little, then add the eggs and cream, stirring it; add pepper and salt to your taste.

Mrs. Cornelia Beer.

CONNECTICUT BAKED BEANS.

Wash the beans and soak them over night. In the morning, pour off the water and pour on fresh; let them simmer on the stove for half an hour, changing the water twice; pour off the water and turn them into a saucepan, with a piece of salt pork, and cook until the beans are soft; score the pork on top and place in the middle of a deep baking dish; pour the beans around it, leaving the pork a little higher than the beans; add enough of the water they were boiled in to moisten. Bake until nicely browned.

Mrs. O. D. Filley.

BOILED GREEN PEAS.

Wash the pods before shelling; then wash and drain the peas after they are shelled; put into a saucepan the pods and cook about thirty minutes; then drain out the pods and put in peas and cook twenty minutes; season with salt and a teaspoon of sugar; let them boil quickly over a brisk fire, with the lid of the saucepan uncovered. When tender pour them into a cullender; put them into a vegetable dish, and in the centre of the peas place a piece of butter. Mint may be added with the peas if desired.

STEWED GREEN PEAS.

Shell one quart of peas, add one onion and one lettuce, cut into slices; put into a stewpan, with butter, pepper and salt, but no more water than that which hangs around the lettuce from washing. Stew gently for one hour; then stir into it a well beaten egg and half a teaspoonful of powdered sugar. When thickened serve: do not allow them to boil after the egg is added.

GREEN PEAS A LA FRANCAISE.

Shell enough peas to make two quarts; put them in cold water, with three ounces of butter, and stir them about until they are well covered with the butter; drain in a cullender; put them in a stewpan with a bunch of parsley and half a dozen green onions; dredge over them a little flour; stir the peas well and moisten with boiling water; boil them quickly over a hot fire for twenty minutes, or until there is no liquor remaining. Dip a small lump of sugar into some water, that it may soon melt; put it in with the peas, adding half a teaspoonful of salt. Take a piece of butter the size of a walnut; work it together with a teaspoonful of flour, and add this to the peas, which should be boiling when it is put in. Keep shaking the stewpan, and when the peas are nicely thickened dress them in a high dish and serve.

EGGS.

TO KEEP EGGS THROUGHOUT THE WINTER.

Wash the eggs clean; have a nice clean box or butter firkin, put a layer of coarse salt, place the eggs in it with small end down; do not let the eggs touch each other; then another layer of salt, so on, until you have packed all your eggs, making the last layer of salt; keep your box well covered.   MISS E. L. GLOVER.

TO PRESERVE EGGS.

Rub each one in salt butter, till every pore of the shell is closed, then pack in dry bran with the small end down, and put in a cool place. Fresh eggs thus treated will keep eight or ten months.

TO BOIL EGGS.

Have ready a saucepan of boiling water; put the eggs into it gently with a spoon, so that they may not crack; for those who like eggs lightly boiled, three minutes will be found sufficient, four minutes will set the whites nicely; and, if liked hard, six to seven minutes will not be too long. Eggs for salad should be boiled from ten to fifteen minutes, and should be placed in a basin of cold water for a few minutes; they should then be rolled on the table with the hand, and the shell will peel off easily.

POACHED EGGS.

Drop fresh eggs in boiling water; when slightly cooked skim out and lay on slices of buttered toast; sprinkle a little salt and pepper on each egg, and a small piece of butter, before serving.

BAKED EGGS.

Butter a dish well, and break the eggs very carefully on it; put on the top of each a little pepper and salt, and a little butter, and put them into a slow oven until well set; serve them hot.

FRIED EGGS.

Break the eggs into cups and slip them into a frying pan of boiling dripping or butter. When the whites are set, take them up, drain them from the grease, and trim off the rough edges. Place them in the centre of the dish; and slices of fried bacon round the edge, or the eggs may be served on the bacon.

EGG OMELET.

From five fresh eggs take the whites of three; beat the yolks and two whites until they are very light; then add a half teacup of milk or cream and a little salt; have an omelet pan hot with a little butter in it, pour in the eggs; when done through, spread on the whites, well beaten; brown, fold over the omelet, turn into a hot dish and serve immediately. Beating the eggs, as if for cake, will prevent the toughness so often found in ordinary omelet.

MRS. W. FALLON.

EGG OMELET.

For a family of three or four persons, take about six eggs; beat the yolks and whites separately, very light, then beat them together; season with a little salt and summer savory, if liked; bake them on a griddle, a little at a time, a round cake, then double over; serve quick and hot, as they come up so light that they are apt to fall if left to cool.

MRS. RICHARDS.

A NICE OMELET FOR BREAKFAST.

Beat two eggs, yolks and whites together, in a bowl, until very light; add a teaspoon of corn starch, dissolved in a half teaspoon of milk; beat all well together, for a few minutes;

a little chopped parsley can be added if wished. In making any kind of omelet, salt and pepper should not be added until sent to the table, and to have them perfectly light, and not tough, the ingredients must be well and quickly beaten with a fork. This omelet is enough for three persons.

Mrs. Lewis E. Kline.

OMELET.

Six eggs; whites beaten to a stiff froth; yolks well beaten; one teacup of warm milk, one tablespoonful of melted butter, one tablespoonful of flour, mix smoothly with a little of the milk, one teaspoonful of salt, and a little pepper; add the whites of the eggs after the other ingredients are well mixed; bake very quick in shallow pans.

BREAD OMELET.

Two slices of bread soaked in a cup of milk; six eggs; mash the bread very fine, and beat the eggs with it; fry, by the spoonful, in butter, or bake in a well-buttered pan; when it stiffens, cut in quarters and turn.

OMELET.

One cup of bread crumbs in one cup of milk; when soft, add three eggs, yolks and whites beaten separately; fry them in a little butter, and roll them up as they brown.

Mrs. F. G. Goddard.

EGG OMELET.

Break the eggs and use the same quantity of milk (in bulk); if eight eggs, about two cups of milk; small piece of melted butter, salt, pepper, a tablespoonful of flour, wet first in some milk; beat all together lightly, just enough to break the yolks well, and bake in a buttered dish; serve in the same; should rise very high.   Mrs. H. Waterman.

SCRAMBLED EGGS.

For a family of six, mix eight eggs beaten light, with one small half teacup of milk; a little salt and pepper. Have a little hot lard or butter in a skillet; pour them in and stir quickly to keep them from burning; when done serve in a hot dish.

EGG GEMS.

Mix together chopped meat and bread crumbs, with pepper, salt and butter, and a little milk; fill some buttered gem-pans with the mixture; then break an egg carefully on the top of each; season with a little salt and pepper, sprinkle some very fine cracker crumbs on top. Bake in eight minutes.

MUMBLED EGGS.

Lay some slices of buttered toast in a hot dish before the fire-place; put some butter and a little salt in a saucepan on the fire; break the eggs quickly on the butter, and stir one way with a silver spoon until it solidifies; then remove it from the fire, still stirring, and spread upon the buttered toast; lightly pepper and serve at once.

EGGS ON TOAST.

Put one-half a pint of milk in a cup on the stove; when scalding hot drop in three eggs, a little salt; stir them in the milk, which should be hot enough to cook the eggs in a few moments, and thicken up the milk. Spread on buttered toast. This is a nice way to cook eggs for an invalid.

BREAD AND BISCUITS.

POTATO YEAST.

Boil six or eight potatoes till soft, drain and mash them very smooth; add two-thirds of a cup of flour and table spoonful of sugar. Thin the mixture with cold water till of the consistency of very thick batter; strain through a cullender, and when cool add a small cup of yeast and set in a warm place till light. Keep in a stone jar with cover. A small cup of this yeast is sufficient to raise two quarts of flour.   MRS. J. M. KRUM.

YEAST.

One handful of hops, eight good sized potatoes in two quarts of water; boil until the potatoes are done. Have a pint of flour ready in a pan, and pour the boiling hop water into it, also adding the potatoes, which must be mashed; beat and mix well; then add one tablespoonful of salt, one tablespoonful of sugar, one tablespoonful of ginger; when lukewarm add a cup of yeast, or one and a half yeast cakes; set in a warm place to rise.
    MRS. M. A. FILLEY & MRS. W. MAURICE.

BREAD.

It is almost impossible to give the proportions for making bread, as each family must in some measure be governed by the quantity and number of loaves they will need. The following proportions may be some guide: Take two gallons best wheat flour, sift into a pan or a large wooden bowl kept for that purpose; make a deep hole in the middle of the flour; have ready half a pint of lukewarm water, in winter it may be a little warmer, but not hot or boiling; stir it well into half a pint of strong fresh yeast (if the yeast is homemade you must use from three-quarters to a whole pint); pour it into the hole in the middle of the flour; with a spoon work in the flour round the edges of the liquid, so as to bring in, by degrees, sufficient flour to form a thin batter, which must be well stirred for a minute or two; then scatter a handful of flour over this batter; lay a cloth over the pan; set it in a warm place. This is called sponge. In the morning when the sponge is risen so as to make cracks in the flour over it (which will take four or five hours), scatter over it two tablespoonfuls of salt, and have ready one large tablespoonful of melted lard; add about two quarts of either milk or water, warm, but not hot enough to scald the yeast, and sufficient to wet it; be careful not to put in too much milk or water at once; knead the whole thoroughly for as much as half an hour, as good bread depends much on the kneading, which to do well requires strength and practice; when sufficiently worked, form the dough into a lump in the middle of the pan, scatter a little flour thinly over the top, cover it; set it again to rise; then put your dough on your pastry board (which must be sprinkled with flour), divide into loaves; work into good shape; have your pans nicely greased with lard, put your loaves in, cover with your bread cloth, and let them rise; when light enough, put them in the oven, which must not be too hot; the loaves, to bake well, will take from two to three hours, according to the size; when the loaves are done, wrap each in a clean coarse towel, previously made damp by sprinkling plentifully with water, then stand them upon end to cool slowly. Bread should always be kept wrapped in a cloth and covered from the air in a box with a close lid. If the bread has been mixed over night, and found on tasting to be sour in the morning, dissolve a teaspooonful of soda in a little milk-warm water, and sprinkle it over the dough; let it set half an hour, then knead it.

If you wish biscuit in the morning, take the same quantities as above, going through the same process, and add the salt and lard; work the dough well; let it rise over night.

In the morning kneading your bread, take out what is wanted for biscuit, roll out the dough and cut in biscuit shape: put them in a pan, set by the stove to rise; when light, put in your oven and bake; then take the rest of the dough, work more flour into it; make into loaves.

PARKER HOUSE ROLLS.

Take two quarts of wheat flour; make a hole in the centre: put in a piece of butter size of an egg, a little salt, a tablespoonful white sugar: pour over this a pint of nearly cold boiled milk with half a teacup of yeast. When well raised mould it fifteen minutes and let it rise again; then cut into cakes and rise; when light, flatten each with the rolling pin; put a small piece of butter on top and fold over, or simply rub with butter if made in a long shape; then put into the pans and rise a little more and bake in a quick oven.

MRS. N. W. PERKINS.

LIGHT ROLLS.

One quart of flour, one-half pint of milk that has been boiled and cooled, half a teaspoonful of sugar, a piece of butter half the size of a hen's egg, half a cup of potato yeast, small pinch of salt. This quantity is sufficient for a family of six. If required for breakfast, put the ingredients in a pan, on the afternoon previous, in the following order: First the flour, making a hole in the centre of it, in which put the butter, sugar, salt and milk, and lastly the yeast. Set the pan away without stirring the ingredients until bedtime; then mix, mould and knead on the board for fifteen minutes; let the dough rise until morning, when knead it again for a few minutes; roll out half an inch thick and cut with a biscuit cutter; turn over one corner, putting a little butter under it. Put the rolls in a pan, not too close together, and let them rise for an hour or more until perfectly light, and bake in a quick oven fifteen minutes.

MRS. J. M. KRUM.

FRENCH ROLLS.

Two quarts of flour, one tablespoonful of sugar, one tablespoonful of butter, one teaspoonful of salt; put all in the centre of flour, and pour over one pint of boiling milk; let stand until lukewarm; dissolve one-half a yeast cake in a little milk, and stir in the milk, but do not disturb the flour; let stand until it comes up light; then stir all up together, and let rise again; then roll and cut out with cutter; butter the top and turn one side over the other; put in pans and let rise again; bake twenty minutes.

MRS. F. A. DURGIN.

EGG BISCUIT.

Three quarts of flour, two eggs, one tablespoonful of butter, one and a half of lard, one teacup of yeast; mix with warm milk or water; set to rise in the evening; in the morning roll out; let them rise before baking.

MRS. S. D. GLOVER.

FRENCH BISCUIT.

Four pints of flour, four eggs, one teaspoonful of sugar, one tablespoonful of butter, one teacup of yeast, one pint of sweet milk, salt; knead well, and let it rise; when quite light, roll thin; grease one-half of the surface with lard or butter; fold the other half over it, and cut into biscuits; let it rise again about one hour, in a warm place, and bake quickly.

COFFEE BREAD.

Three quarts of flour, four eggs, one tablespoonful butter, one of lard, one cup sugar, one cup currants, teacup of yeast; mix all together with milk soft enough to work well; the thinner it is the better; water will do if you have not the milk; both must be warm; set to rise. In the morning roll it out in thin cakes; let them rise; before putting them in the oven mix some sugar and cinnamon together; have some hot melted butter and pour it on the cakes, then sprinkle the sugar over it. Bake in a slow oven.

MRS. S. D. GLOVER.

APPLE OR PEACH BREAD.

Before kneading your dough take out what quantity you wish, as it ought not to be as stiff as bread dough; roll thin size of your pan; let it rise; when light, spread with melted butter. Have some nice juicy apples pared and sliced very thin; lay a thick layer of apples sprinkled well with sugar and cinnamon; set it in the oven to bake. Fresh peaches may be done in the same way without the cinnamon.

MISS E. L. GLOVER.

CORN BREAD.

One quart of corn meal, little salt, one teaspoonful soda, butter milk enough to make a thin batter.

BROWN BREAD.

One quart of unbolted flour, three tablespoonfuls of molasses, one level teaspoonful of soda, three-fourths of a pint of butter milk; stir thoroughly and bake two hours, the oven not too hot.

GRAHAM BREAD.

Two quarts of Graham flour, two coffee-cups of golden syrup, salt, and potato yeast enough to make it the right consistency; sift the flour, to make it light, and put the bran back in the flour, tossing it up thoroughly with the salt, before adding the other articles; the potato yeast must be of the best, and put in enough to make the bread without adding any water; mix thoroughly with the hand—the dough should not be stiff enough to knead, neither thin enough to pour out like cake, but between the two—put it in the pan in which it is to be baked, and when it is well risen, bake about an hour and a half. For the above receipt I have a round block-tin pan, that holds four and one-half quarts; the dough should rise quite to the top. This bread, like all nice things, requires several trials to get it just right, but when it is *right*, it makes, with a good cup of coffee, a breakfast fit for a king.

MRS. W. FALLON.

BOSTON BROWN BREAD.

Three cups of Graham flour with bran, three cups of Indian meal, half a cup of molasses, a little salt, three tablespoons of yeast, mixed with three and a half cups of lukewarm water; let it rise about two hours, or until light, then add one teaspoonful of saleratus, and bake five hours, the last three hours in a very slow oven. Mrs. D. R. Powell.

BUNS.

Three cups sweet milk, one cup white sugar, one cup yeast; mix a little thicker than for batter cakes; put to rise over night; in the morning add one cup of butter, one cup of sugar, one nutmeg, one tablespoonful of extract of lemon, half a teaspoonful of soda; mix hard to mould; set to rise; then mould and put into pans and let rise again. Beat up an egg and brush them over with it before baking. Make the buns the size of a small biscuit. Mrs. Wm. Maurice.

RUSKS.

Two teacups of milk, one teacup of yeast, a piece of butter size of an egg; stir in the flour and let it rise; then add two eggs and one cup of sugar; beat well together, then let it rise again; then roll out and cut in small cakes for the oven. Mrs. G. F. Filley.

MRS. R.'S RUSKS.

One pint of mashed potatoes, one cup of sugar, one cup of butter; set with a little yeast the evening before making. Next day take four eggs, another cup of sugar, and flour enough; make in form of biscuit and bake for supper.

MUFFINS.

One quart flour, one pint sweet milk, two eggs, two tablespoonfuls home-made yeast, one tablespoonful sugar, a little salt; set to rise at night; in the morning add two tablespoonfuls melted butter. Fill the pans and let it stand a short time before baking; it is important to add the butter after rising. Mrs. S. A. Ranlett.

DROP MUFFINS.

One quart of flour, two eggs, a full tablespoon of butter, two tablespoons of yeast, and milk sufficient to make a very stiff batter, stiff enough to let a spoon stand up in it; beat very light and set to rise; drop them one spoonful in a place and bake quickly.

RYE MUFFINS.

One quart flour, two cups rye meal, one-half cup yeast, salt; mix with water to a very thick batter; one-half teaspoon soda (dissolved), well beaten in, after it is raised. Bake in rings.   Mrs. W. Maurice.

DELICATE CORN MUFFINS.

Two eggs, two tablespoons white sugar, beaten together; add three cups flour with two teaspoons yeast powder sifted through it, one heaping tablespoon of Indian meal, one cup of milk, one tablespoon of melted butter, a little salt. Bake in hot iron roll pans, well buttered, fifteen minutes. This will make one dozen.   Mrs. R. S. Frost, Boston.

GRAHAM FLOUR MUFFINS.

To a pint of sour milk add soda sufficient to correct the acid only, a little salt, one tablespoonful of white sugar; use two-thirds Graham flour to one-third white flour; stir into the milk sufficient to make a batter a little thicker than for griddle cakes; beat thoroughly, and bake in a hot oven. N. B.—Heat the bake-pans hot before filling.
                                     Mrs. S. A. Ranlett.

MUFFINS.

To one quart of milk put in one tablespoonful of butter, and put on the stove to warm, then add one-half teacup of yeast, a little salt and flour to make stiff; let it stand until morning, then put into rings; let it stand a few moments, then bake.   Mrs. C. B. Richards.

SOUR MILK MUFFINS.

One and a half pints sour milk, three tablespoonfuls butter (melted), one tablespoonful white sugar, one teaspoonful soda, two eggs, eight pints flour. MRS. W. MAURICE.

MUFFINS.

One quart of flour, one egg, three tablespoonfuls of sugar, three tablespoonfuls of cream, or a piece of butter half the size of an egg, milk enough to make a batter soft as pancakes, one teaspoonful of soda, two teaspoonfuls of cream of tartar; bake quickly. MRS. T. T. RICHARDS.

MUFFINS.

Two eggs beaten together light, one pint of milk, one and a half teaspoonfuls of sugar, a little salt, flour enough to make a batter about as stiff as cake, two teaspoonfuls of yeast powder, a piece of butter half the size of an egg.
MAGGIE FANNING.

SALLY LUNN.

Two eggs, one cup of sugar, a piece of butter the size of an egg, a coffee-cup of milk, two teaspoonfuls of cream of tartar, one teaspoonful of soda, flour enough to make a thick batter; bake in a quick oven. MRS. W. H. PULSIFER.

SALLY LUNN.

Beat three eggs very light, one pint of warm milk, half a teacup of butter, half a teacup of yeast, two pints of flour, one teaspoonful and a half of salt; beat well together, and pour into a buttered pan in which it is to be baked; when light bake with a quick heat. You can add to this a teacup of sugar if desired. MRS. T. J. ALBRIGHT, Kirkwood.

GRAHAM ROLLS.

Mix sponge of white flour at night; in the morning add one teacup of milk, one tablespoonful of butter, three tablespoonfuls of sugar, one-half white flour, one-half Graham, with bran; mix, knead and rise until light; roll out, spread lightly with butter, make in rolls, and bake when light.
MRS. D. R. POWELL.

GRAHAM ROLLS.

One quart of Graham flour, one pint of wheat flour, two tablespoonfuls of lard, two tablespoonfuls of sugar, half cup of yeast, water enough to make stiff as pound-cake; set to rise over night; bake in little pound-cake tins twenty minutes.   MRS. LEWIS E. KLINE.

SODA BISCUIT.

One quart of flour, two tablespoons of butter, one teaspoon of salt, one of soda, two of cream of tartar; use sufficient milk to make a soft dough, about one-half pint. If made with sour milk, leave out the cream of tartar.

CREAM BISCUIT.

Four eggs to a quart of milk; a piece of butter as large as an egg, a little salt, sixteen tablespoons of flour; beat your eggs very light; bake in teacups or patty-pans. To be eaten hot.

BRIGHTON BISCUIT.

One cup of butter, two cups of powdered sugar, beaten to a cream, one cup of milk and one teaspoonful of soda, a little nutmeg, and flour enough to roll very thin; sift sugar over them and bake in a quick oven.

BOLT BISCUIT.

One pound of flour, one pound of sugar, quarter of a pound of butter, four eggs, one nutmeg, about as much as a good sized teaspoon will do for a cake.   MRS. BROCK.

CAKES WITHOUT EGGS.

Five cups of flour, two of sugar, one of butter, one nutmeg; make up with milk, and work in a biscuit break till it blisters; add a desert spoon of soda.

BEAT BISCUIT.

One quart of flour, two tablespoons of lard, a little milk; beat or pound with a roller thoroughly until very light; add salt.

BUNS.

Three cups of milk, one cup of sugar, one cup yeast; thicken with flour, like batter; rise till very light, then add a teaspoonful of soda, one cup more of sugar, one cup of melted butter; thicken to the consistency of biscuit, scatter in a few currants; rise again, roll out; make them about three-quarters of an inch thick; cut in squares, put them into your pan, and let them rise again.   C. G. HILL.

DIXIE BISCUIT. "DELICIOUS."

Three pints of flour, two eggs, two tablespoons of lard, one cup of yeast, one cup of milk; mix at eleven o'clock, roll out at four o'clock, and cut with two sizes of cutters, putting the smaller one on top; let rise until supper. Bake twenty minutes.   MRS. F. A. LANE.

MILK BISCUIT. "SPLENDID."

Two pounds of flour, one-quarter of a pound of lard, one teacup of yeast, one teaspoon of salt, one pint of milk; make a soft dough, and set at ten o'clock; stir at three; at five, mould into biscuit, adding more flour; let rise until supper. Bake twenty minutes.   MRS. F. A. LANE.

POP-OVERS.

Four eggs beaten hard three minutes in one quart of milk, one teaspoonful of salt; stir in nine pop-over cups of flour; beat all well, and finally add another pint of milk; to this last pint of milk you may add a teacup of boiled rice; pour into cups half full of batter; start with a very hot oven; one hour to bake, and serve instantly.
  MRS. J. G. CHAPMAN.

PUFFS, OR POP-OVERS.

Four cups of milk, four eggs, four cups of flour, a little salt; bake half an hour, and let stand in the oven with door open another half hour; fill the cups about half full.
  MRS. PRICE.

TEA CAKE.

One quart of flour, a little salt, break four eggs into the flour, a small cup of melted butter, two tablespoonfuls of powdered sugar, three gills of milk; bake one hour in small cups. MRS. W. H. PULSIFER.

SOFT CAKE.

Three eggs, one pint of milk, salt, flour sufficient to make a thick batter; bake in two cakes; split and butter while hot; lay the brown side against the buttered, so as to soften the crust. MRS. WM. MAURICE.

SHORT CAKE.

Six cups of flour, two cups of milk, two eggs beaten and mixed in the milk, a piece of butter the size of an egg, half a cup of sugar, two teaspoonfuls of cream of tartar, one teaspoonful of soda, a little salt.

SHORT CAKE.

One quart of flour, two teaspoonfuls of yeast powder mixed with the flour, a large tablespoonful of butter, milk to make a soft dough; bake quickly, split open, butter and add fruit, mixed with sugar.

DROP CAKES.

One quart of sweet milk, three eggs well beaten, one quart of flour, a little salt; bake in gem-pans, in a hot oven; heat the pans before using. MRS. D. C. YOUNG.

KIRKWOOD PUFFS.

Four eggs, the whites and yolks beaten separately, very light; one quart of sweet cream, or one quart of milk, and butter the size of an egg, three teaspoonfuls of Price's cream baking powder, one-half a teaspoon of salt, and twenty tablespoonfuls of flour. MRS. M. A. GARDNER.

INDIAN CUP CAKE.

One pint of milk, three-fourths of a pint of wheat flour, one-fourth of a pint of corn meal, two eggs, a tablespoonful of butter, a little salt; bake three-quarters of an hour, in cups that have been warmed.   MRS. CHAS. JONES.

CORN CAKES.

Three eggs well beaten, one quart of sour milk, one large teaspoon of soda, one cup of flour, a little salt and sugar; beat in enough corn meal to make a stiff batter. Makes two dozen, muffin shape.
MRS. PALMER HAMPTON.

WHEAT GEMS.

Five cups of flour, one quart of milk, two eggs, very little salt; bake in gem-pan, heating the pan before filling.

SPANISH BUNS.

Three-quarters of a pound of sugar, one-half pound of flour, one-quarter of a pound of butter, four eggs, two and one-half wine glasses of cream; beat the cream and butter while warm, add the sugar, the yolks of eggs and flour, then the whites; dissolve a tablespoon of yeast powder in a wine-glass of rosewater, and add just before putting into the oven.

CENTER HARBOR CAKES.

Take three eggs, beat them very light, separately, beat in flour enough to make a thin batter; add salt and a piece of butter the size of half an egg; then take a pint of milk and some flour, and add them alternately, until you make a batter almost as thick as for muffins; have one of Waterman's patent pans for baking batter cake, warmed and greased. It will take twenty minutes in a moderate oven to bake them.   MRS. HUGH CAMPBELL.

ANNIE'S WAFFLES.

Take two eggs, one quart of flour, one tablespoon of butter, one pint of sweet milk, two teaspoons yeast powder, a little salt; mix very lightly, bake in waffle irons; muffins can be made as above, only a little thicker, and add a spoonful of sugar and bake in the oven in rings.

WAFFLES.

One tablespoon of lard melted in a tin pan on the stove; when hot, not scalding, stir in one tablespoon of corn meal; when cold, stir in one quart sweet milk, one teaspoon of soda, one pint of flour with two teaspoons cream tartar, one egg, salt, a thin batter; add more flour if necessary. Have the waffle iron hot. MRS. D. T. WALES.

WAFFLES.

Six eggs, one quart of milk, one-fourth pound of butter, one-fourth pound of powdered sugar, one and a half pounds of flour, one teaspoon of powdered cinnamon; warm the milk slightly; cut up the butter in it and stir it a little; beat the eggs well and pour them into the butter and milk, and sprinkle in half the flour gradually; stir in the sugar by degrees. MRS. LEWIS E. KLINE.

BATTER CAKES.

One coffee-cup of sour milk, two eggs well beaten (either separately or together), flour sufficient to make a good batter; just before baking add one teaspoon of soda, dissolved in a little water.

CORN MEAL GRIDDLE CAKES.

One pint of meal mixed with four teaspoonfuls of flour, one pint of milk, four eggs, a little salt, one teaspoonful soda, and two of cream tartar. It is much nicer to beat the whites of the eggs very light, and to stir them in the last minute before baking.

BUCKWHEAT CAKES.

Two handfuls of corn meal mixed with about one quart warm water, and not quite one-half cup of yeast, two tablespoons molasses, a little salt, and buckwheat to stiffen pretty stiff; put in a warm place to rise; mix in an earthen crock and leave some in the bottom to serve as a sponge for the next morning instead of getting fresh yeast.

Mrs. E. F. Richards.

SQUASH GRIDDLE CAKES.

One cup squash (strained), one cup of milk, one egg, salt, one teaspoon sugar, piece of soda size of a pea; flour enough to make a batter not very stiff. Mrs. T. T. Richards.

RICE CAKES.

Have your rice thoroughly boiled, then make a batter of two eggs beat up light, one pint of sweet milk, flour enough to stiffen not very stiff, half a teaspoonful of soda and one of cream of tartar, then stir in rice enough to stiffen well, and beat up with a fork.

CORN CAKES.

One egg, one pint of sour milk, one-third of a teaspoonful of soda, corn meal; stir the soda with the egg, then add the milk, and last the flour and a little salt; bake on griddles.

STALE BREAD GRIDDLE CAKES.

Take stale bread, soak it in water until soft; strain off the water through a cullender; beat the bread crumbs lightly with a fork; to one quart of the soaked crumbs add one quart of milk, one quart of flour, and four eggs; bake on a griddle.

MOCK BUCKWHEAT CAKES.

Two-thirds of a cup of yeast, two quarts of batter made of warm water and wheat flour stirred together the night before, same as buckwheat; add a small pinch of soda in the morning.

GREEN CORN GRIDDLE CAKES.

Twelve ears of corn, to be cut off and chopped fine, two cups of milk, one cup of flour, three eggs and salt.

PEA FRITTERS.

Cook a pint more peas than you need for dinner; mash while hot with a wooden spoon; put by until morning; make a batter of two whipped eggs, a cupful of milk, quarter of a teaspoonful of soda, half a teaspoonful of cream of tartar, and half a cup of flour; stir the pea mixture into this, beating very hard, and cook like ordinary griddle cakes.

MRS. WILSON'S CORN BREAD.

One quart of corn meal, one spoonful of lard, scald with boiling water; stir well two teaspoons of salt, three eggs well beaten, a little soda in sour milk enough to make thin batter, or two teaspoons of yeast powder with sweet milk.

MRS. STODDARD'S CORN BREAD.

Three eggs, one cup of milk, two teaspoonfuls baking powder, mixed in a little milk, two cups corn meal, one cup soft boiled rice, a little salt, butter the size of a walnut. Bake in a quick oven.

BANNOCK.

Scant pint of corn meal, one quart of milk, six eggs and a little salt; scald half the milk and mix with the meal while hot; add the other half cold; to this add the eggs well beaten, and bake three-quarters of an hour.

BLUEBERRY CAKE.

One small cup of sugar, half a cup of butter, and yolks of three eggs beaten to a cream, one teaspoon even full of soda dissolved in a cup and a half of sweet milk, and flour enough for cake batter, with two teaspoonfuls of cream of tartar in the flour, then the whites of three eggs beaten to a stiff froth; dredge a quart of blueberries or huckleberries and stir into the mixture just before putting into the baking pan; bake quickly.   MRS. C. B. RICHARDS.

DUTCH TOAST.

One pint of milk and two eggs, sweeten; add a little nutmeg; cut in thin slices baker's bread; dip in the custard and fry brown. MRS. W. H. PULSIFER.

STRAWBERRY SHORT CAKE.

One quart of flour, three eggs, one tablespoonful of melted butter, two teaspoonfuls of yeast powder, milk enough to make a batter, and bake in jelly-cake pans; when done, butter, and put fresh strawberries between the layers of cake, and sprinkle each with sugar.
MRS. JOSEPH SHIPPEN.

STRAWBERRY SHORT CAKE.

Make a dough the same as for soda biscuit; roll it thin, the size of your jelly-cake pans; bake it, and when done open the cakes and butter both the inside and outside layers; have your strawberries nicely picked and sugared before you prepare the dough, in order to have plenty of juice; spread your berries in both the upper and lower layer, putting one layer on top of the other; set it again in the oven for a few moments, not long enough to cook the berries.
MRS. E. L. GLOVER.

WHORTLEBERRY CAKE.

One cup of sour milk, one small cup of sugar, one tablespoonful of butter, one egg, one teaspoonful of soda; flour as stiff as ordinary cake; as many berries as you please, nearly a quart to this rule. MRS. T. T. RICHARDS.

BOSTON BROWN BREAD.

One cup of corn meal, one cup of rye meal, one cup of flour, half a cup of molasses, half a teaspoonful of salt, and a teaspoonful of soda; mix to a stiff batter, with sour milk; put it in a tin pail, cover tightly, and boil in a pot of water four hours. MRS. E. P. PETTES.

BOSTON BROWN BREAD.

Three cups of yellow corn meal, two and one-half cups of rye meal, both unsifted, one cup of hot water, three cups of new milk, one cup of molasses, one large teaspoonful of soda, one teaspoonful of salt; stir well; steam three and one-half hours. MRS. H. N. DAVIS.

STEAMED BROWN BREAD.

One pint of corn meal, one half pint of rye, three cups of milk, two eggs, two teaspoonfuls of yeast powder, little salt; steam two and one-half hours, then set in oven one-half an hour. Eat while hot. MRS. DERGANS.

BOSTON BROWN BREAD.

Three cups of corn meal, two cups of rye meal, one cup of molasses, one quart of water, one teaspoonful of soda; steam three hours. When coarse rye cannot be obtained, use stale bread, chopped fine, in about equal quantities, with the corn meal. MISS ELIZA FREEBORN.

BOILED BREAD.
(TO BE EATEN WARM, WITH ROAST MEATS, AT DINNER.)

One cup of Graham flour, two cups of corn meal, teaspoon of soda, teaspoon of salt, tablespoon of molasses, pint and a half of sour milk; boil in mould three hours, closely covered. Same can be made with sweet milk and yeast powder. MRS. WELLS.

PUDDINGS.

PLUM PUDDING.

One square loaf of baker's bread (weight about ten ounces), cut in thin slices, with crusts trimmed off, and buttered on both sides. Sprinkle the bottom of a stone crock with fine layer raisins, then put in a layer of the buttered bread, cover with a layer of raisins, clean dried currants and citron cut fine, some New Orleans brown sugar, a little ground nutmeg, cinnamon, and a very little cloves; fill your crock until within an inch of the top, making the top layer of bread. Then take three pints of milk, let it come to a boil in a milk boiler, add to it six eggs well beaten, one cup of sugar, teaspoonful of salt, one-half pint of molasses; pour over the pudding and thoroughly mix by cutting through to the bottom with a knife; bake three hours in a slow oven, let stand an hour, keeping hot, before turning upside down into the pudding dish. Served with sauce.

RICHARDS.

STEAM PLUM PUDDING.

One cup of suet chopped fine, one cup of molasses, one cup of milk, two eggs, two cups of chopped raisins, one cup of currants, one-quarter of a pound of citron, one teaspoonful each of soda, salt, cloves, allspice, ginger; one-half of a nutmeg, two teaspoonfuls of cinnamon, flour enough to make a stiff batter. Steam three hours.

SAUCE.—Half a cup of butter, one cup of sugar, the yolk of one egg, beaten to a cream, one glass of wine; heat it slowly; when ready for the table beat the white of the egg very light, and put it on top of the sauce.

MRS. H. C. MOORE.

BAKED ENGLISH PLUM PUDDING.

One-quarter of a pound of suet chopped fine, half a teaspoonful of salt, six soda crackers or half a pound of bread crumbs, one-half pound stoned raisins, wet and dredged with flour, half a pound of currants, half a pound of sugar, three ounces of citron, one quart of milk, six eggs, two grated nutmegs, one tablespoonful of mace and cinnamon, half gill of brandy. Steam two hours, and brown half an hour in oven. MRS. R. H. MORTON.

PLUM PUDDING.

Two quarts of best flour, two pounds of raisins, two pounds of currants, one-half pound of citron, one pound of suet, two nutmegs, one gill of brandy, sugar to suit taste; the whole to be made up with milk. Boil well four hours.
MRS. L. E. KLINE.

PLUM PUDDING.

One loaf of bread, one quart of milk, one-half pound of sugar, one-half pint of molasses, one-quarter of a pound of butter or suet, six eggs, one teaspoon of cinnamon, cloves, allspice, one small bowl raisins, salt to your taste.
MRS. T. T. RICHARDS.

PLUM PUDDING.

One cup of raisins, one cup of currants, and one cup of suet chopped fine, three cups of flour, three eggs, two teaspoonfuls of baking powder. Put suet and fruit into the flour dry, also baking powder, then break in the eggs; add milk enough to make a batter still enough for cake; spice to taste; a few pieces of citron sliced very fine may be added. Boil three hours in a mould or floured bag; serve with wine sauce. MRS. D. R. POWELL.

BLACK PUDDING.

Eight eggs, half a cup of butter, one cup of flour, one cup of sugar, one cup of milk, one pint of molasses, one gill of brandy, one nutmeg. Beat the eggs and butter together, then the flour until smooth, then the other ingredients; lastly, one large teaspoonful of soda; or better, put the soda in the molasses. Better partly steamed, then baked. Take a full hour to cook, or bake one hour. For sauce, beat butter and sugar together to a froth and pour a little boiling water over it. A very rich pudding.

Mrs. R. H. Morton.

PLUM PUDDING.

One loaf of baker's bread grated, three pints of milk, one cup of molasses, one cup of sugar, one cup of butter, one pound of raisins stoned, six eggs, mixed, spice to taste, one teaspoonful of soda. Bake two hours and a half in a moderate oven.

Miss A. M. Smiley.

ENGLISH PLUM PUDDING.

Beat the yolks and whites of ten eggs very light, stir in a cup of sugar, one-half pound of chopped suet, one-half teaspoonful of ground cloves, same of cinnamon, the grated peel of a lemon, the inside of a French loaf of bread picked to crumbs, and two teaspoonfuls of yeast powder; dredge half a pound of candied orange peel, same of citron cut in slices, one pound of seeded raisins, one pound of currants washed and dried well; stir all together and put in a piece of cloth; tie perfectly tight at first to give it a good shape; after boiling fifteen or twenty minutes loosen the string and put back to boil. Serve with rich sauce.

Mrs. Frank Filley.

SUET PUDDING.

Six eggs, small bowl of suet chopped fine, one cup of sour milk, one teaspoonful of soda, flour as stiff as you can beat it, one bowl of raisins, or more, a little sugar; cover the pudding, and boil constantly two hours and a half, or if steamed three hours; boil in a drilling bag; cover with butter and flour before putting the pudding into boil.

Mrs. R. H. Morton.

BOILED SUET PUDDING.

Two teacups of flour, one of suet, two tablespoonfuls of sugar, half a teaspoonful of soda, wet with milk.
Mrs. G. F. Filley.

SUET PUDDING.

One cup of chopped suet, one cup of molasses, one cup of water, one cup of raisins, one cup of currants, three and a half cups of flour, two teaspoonfuls of baking powder; if any is left it can be steamed over; will be better the second day; to be served with a warm sauce. Steam three or four hours.
Mrs. S. Copp and Many Others.

PRESIDENT'S PUDDING.

Two-thirds of a cup of sugar, two large tablespoonfuls of butter, the yolks of four eggs well beaten, crumb half a loaf of baker's bread fine; add the rind and juice of one large lemon, one teaspoonful of vanilla; mix all together; then put half in the bottom of a pudding dish; spread on this a very little of preserves or fresh fruit, then put in the remainder of the mixture; bake half an hour; whip the whites of the four eggs, with half a cup of fine sugar and a teaspoonful of vanilla spread over it.
Mrs. D. Young.

BREAD PUDDING.

One quart of milk, one pint of bread crumbs, half a cup of butter, four eggs, one cup of sugar; beat milk and butter; add the yolks of eggs and sugar beaten, with a little cold milk, thin the bread, put in the oven, and add the whites of the eggs, well beaten, just before taking out.

APPLE BREAD PUDDING.

Three eggs beaten separately, beat the yolks in a pint of milk, break in dry bread, a little salt, a small cup of sugar; stir in two apples sliced fine, the whites of the eggs last; bake one hour.
Mrs. T. E. Kline.

BREAD AND BUTTER PUDDING.

Cut some slices of bread moderately thick, without the crust, butter, and cover the bottom of a buttered dish with them; spread a pound of currants, raisins, or stewed apples over the slices, strew some brown sugar over it; put another layer of bread and fruit, etc., with a layer of bread for the top, then pour over the whole four eggs, mixed with a pint of milk; bake one hour; grate nutmeg over it when done; serve warm.

PUDDING FRUIT.

Take apple sauce or stewed pears, or peaches, or any kind of small berries, and mix them with equal quantities of rusk crumbs; make a custard of four eggs, one quart of milk, sweetening very sweet; mix it with the crumbs and bake twenty minutes. MRS. D. YOUNG.

BREAD MERINGUE.

Rub stale bread (for a small family about a pint); add milk to make a little thicker than custard, lump of butter the size of an egg, yolks of four eggs, sweetened; let it bake until a light brown; take it out and cover up with jelly, any kind you like; beat the whites of eggs, flavor and sweeten, spread over the top; bake a few minutes; eat cold. Some serve with cream. MRS. BROCK.

BAKED INDIAN PUDDING.

Boil one quart of milk and one pint of fine Indian meal, stirring it well; mix three tablespoonfuls of flour with one pint of milk until free from lumps; mix this with the Indian meal and stir the mixture well. When moderately warm, stir in three beaten eggs, two spoonfuls of sugar, one teaspoonful of salt, two of cinnamon or nutmeg, and one tablespoonful of melted butter. When baked five or six minutes stir in raisins and one-half pint of milk.

MRS. S. R. FILLEY.

BAKED INDIAN PUDDING. No. 2.

One quart of milk boiled, seven spoonfuls of corn meal, one cup of molasses, one teaspoon of salt, one-half cup of cold milk put in without stirring, just before baking.

Mrs. Wm. Maurice.

BOILED INDIAN PUDDING.

Three pints of milk, ten heaping tablespoons of sifted corn meal, one-half pint of molasses, two eggs; scald the meal with the milk; add the molasses and a teaspoon of salt; put in the eggs when it is cool enough not to scald them, put in one tablespoon of ginger. Tie the bag so that it will be two-thirds full of the pudding in order to give room to swell. Suet improves it.

CORN MEAL PUDDING.

One pint of milk, one-half pint of corn meal, one-fourth pound of brown sugar, one-fourth pound of butter; mix the above and boil in the milk until the meal is scalded; when cool, put in a little salt, the yolks of four eggs; beat the whites to a stiff froth and stir in lightly; dredge with dried bread crumbs; put in the pudding bag and boil two hours.

Mrs. Wm. Maurice.

RICE PUDDING.

Boil a coffee-cup of rice in a quart of milk, and a little salt, until the milk is entirely absorbed, then stir in the grated rind and juice of a lemon, four large spoonfuls of white sugar, two tablespoonfuls of butter, the yolks of four eggs. Bake in a buttered dish three-quarters of an hour, then beat the whites of four eggs with twelve dessert spoonfuls of white sugar to a stiff froth, spread over the top, and bake a light brown.

Mrs. G. Leighton and Mrs. J. Lewis.

WASHINGTON PUDDING.

Boil one cup of rice in one pint of water till the water has all boiled away, then add a quart of milk and boil till it

PUDDINGS. 115

thickens, stirring it carefully all the time; then add the yolks of three eggs well beaten, the grated rind of one lemon, and eight tablespoonfuls of sugar. Pour this into a dish, and let it stand while the whites of the three eggs are beaten to a stiff froth, to which add eight tablespoonfuls of powdered sugar, the juice of the lemon, beat all well together; pour the icing over the pudding, set it in a moderate oven, and watch till it is baked a light brown.

MRS. BROCK.

A DELICIOUS RICE PUDDING.

Take two quarts of sweet milk, two heaping tablespoonfuls of rice, a teacup of raisins, a little salt and sugar to suit the taste; grate in about half a nutmeg, stir all together cold, put into the oven and bake slowly for about two hours, or until it becomes creamy. It is best eaten cold.

MRS. GARDINER.

TAPIOCA PUDDING.

One cup of tapioca soaked over night in water or milk, one quart of milk, four eggs, five tablespoonfuls of sugar; let the milk come to a boil, then add one whole egg and the yolks of three beaten light, and the sugar; boil until thick; pour into your pudding dish, and add the whites of three eggs beaten to a froth, with one tablespoonful of sugar; bake a few moments to brown lightly the top: flavor to your taste; lemon is nice. MRS. R. H. MORTON.

TAPIOCA PUDDING.

Two and a half tablespoonfuls of tapioca put in a tin pan with half a pint of milk, put on the stove to soften for an hour and a half, beat up one egg, add a little sugar; beat up light, then add a little milk and raisins; beat all together; put in a baking dish in the oven for half an hour.

MRS. E. F. RICHARDS.

LEMON TAPIOCA PUDDING.

Take a teacup of large tapioca and soak it over night in a pint of water; in the morning make a rich lemonade with two or three lemons and a pint of water, put it with the tapioca, and boil until clear; if too thick, add more water; peel the lemons very thin, cut the peel into straws, and boil until tender, then drain off the water and add the peel to the tapioca before quite done. To be eaten cold, with cream.

MRS. WM. MAURICE.

TAPIOCA WITH APPLES.

Six tablespoonfuls of sugar, five tablespoonfuls of tapioca, eight apples, two quarts of water; flavor with lemon; melt in a dish; add water; bake one hour and a half.

HUNTINGTON PUDDING.

One quart of milk, one cup of tapioca, three eggs, eight tablespoonfuls of sugar, butter the size of an egg; bake twenty minutes, and then pour upon it a frosting made of eight tablespoonfuls of sugar, whites of three eggs, juice of one lemon; bake till slightly brown.

MRS. WENTWORTH.

BLACKBERRY TAPIOCA.

Half a teacup of tapioca, wash it nicely, and let it stand in a bowl full of water, with a little salt, till it swells, then let it boil slowly till all is dissolved and clear like starch, adding water till it is about the same consistency, and add a little white sugar; stew the berries with brown sugar, then take a dish and put a layer of tapioca while hot, and one of berries, till the dish is full, then set it in the oven about ten minutes. Eat cold, with cream and sugar.

Prepare the tapioca in the same way; put a layer of that and one of cut and sugared peaches, instead of the berries, is very nice; but the peaches do not need any cooking but what they get in the oven. Raspberries are delicious done the same way. MRS. BROCK.

STRAWBERRY TAPIOCA.

Soak over night a large cupful of tapioca in cold water; in the morning put half of it in a baking dish, sprinkle sugar over the tapioca, then on this put a quart of berries, sugar, and the rest of the tapioca, cover about a quarter of an inch with water: bake in a moderate oven until it looks clear; in baking, if it seems too dry, more water is needed. Eat with cream or custard. Make peach tapioca in the same way, using less water and cooking longer.

Mrs. E. H. Semple.

PINEAPPLE TAPIOCA.

Pare and grate the fruit, allowing one pineapple to two cups of tapioca, mixing the fruit and sugar thoroughly.

Mrs. E. H. Semple.

BATTER PUDDING.

One quart of milk, six eggs, nine tablespoonfuls of flour, a little salt. Separate the eggs, beat the yolks, pour into the milk, stir in the flour, and last of all beat the whites to a froth and bake immediately.

Mrs. S. C. Davis.

STEAMED BATTER PUDDING.

One quart of sweet milk, one pint and a half of flour, two teaspoonfuls of yeast powder, two eggs, and a little salt. Mix in a batter, put in a bucket and set in a pot of boiling water. Boil one hour and a half.

NICE BATTER PUDDING.

One quart of milk, half a pint of flour, seven eggs beaten separately, a little salt, one tablespoonful of melted butter. Bake three-quarters of an hour.

Miss E. Tucker.

BOILED FLOUR PUDDING.

Ten tablespoonfuls of sifted flour, five eggs, one and a half pints of milk, one small teaspoonful of salt; beat the eggs and milk together, and stir them into the flour gradually; tie in a bag, not too tight; boil two hours and a quarter.

Mrs. Brock.

FEATHER CAKE PUDDING.

Two cups of sugar, one cup of sweet milk, three cups of flour, one-half cup of butter, three eggs, three teaspoonfuls of baking powder. Mrs. D. Young.

COTTAGE PUDDING.

One cup of sugar, the yolks of two eggs well beaten, one cup of sweet milk, three tablespoonfuls of melted butter, one teaspoonful of soda (dissolved), two teaspoonfuls of cream of tartar rubbed dry into one pint of flour, the grated rind of one lemon; mix well; bake half an hour. Sauce for the above: The whites of two eggs beaten, with one cup of sugar and the juice of one lemon. Mrs. S. A. Ranlett.

PUFF PUDDINGS.

One pint of milk, one pint of flour, three eggs, a little salt. Bake in cups fifteen or twenty minutes; serve with wine sauce. Miss Krum.

GERMAN PUFFS.

Five eggs, leaving out the whites of three; five tablespoonfuls of flour; one tablespoonful of melted butter; one pint of sweet milk. Beat the eggs and milk together till quite light, then add flour and butter. Bake in cups half full; will be baked in fifteen minutes. Sauce: Beat the whites of three eggs to a stiff froth, add the juice of two lemons mixed in a cup of powdered sugar, stir well with the eggs; place the puffs in a dish, letting them cool a little, and pour the sauce over them. Mrs. J. G. Chapman.

SPONGE PUDDING.

One quart of milk, quarter pound of butter, quarter pound of flour, quarter pound of sugar, ten eggs. Beat the sugar, butter and flour smooth, beat the eggs separately, then put the yolks in; let the milk come to a boil and pour over the butter, sugar, flour and eggs; beat the whites to a stiff froth, and stir in quickly. Bake half an hour in a pan of water. Mrs. Wm. Maurice.

PUDDINGS.

SPONGE PUDDING.

One tablespoonful of milk, one cup of flour, one cup of sugar, one teaspoonful of baking powder, three eggs. Beat yolks of eggs and sugar together light, then add flour and white of eggs beaten very light, add milk; put the baking powder in the flour; steam in cups twenty minutes. This will make seven cups; to be eaten with a rich sauce.
MRS. D. R. POWELL.

SUNDERLAND PUDDING.

Eight eggs, five heaping tablespoonfuls of flour, pint and a half of milk, a pinch of salt. Beat the yolks well, and mix smoothly with the flour, then add the milk; lastly beat the whites to a stiff froth, beat all well, and bake at once. Sauce for the above: Ten tablespoonfuls of white sugar, butter size of an egg, one egg, one wine-glass of water. Beat the egg and sugar well together, have the water boil and stir in the butter, pour into the beaten egg and sugar, add a wine-glass of wine, and send to table at once. This should be a perfect foam when made. Bake in cups.
MRS. H. McKITTRICK.

KISS PUDDING.

One quart of milk, three and a half heaping tablespoons of corn starch, five eggs, one-half cup of sugar, a little salt; boil the milk and stir in the corn starch, wet with a little of the cold milk; then add the sugar, salt, and the beaten yolks of the eggs; let it boil a few minutes; flavor, pour into a dish and smooth nicely. Beat the whites of the eggs to a stiff froth; stir in one-half cup of powdered sugar; flavor if you choose; turn it upon the pudding and set in the oven for a few minutes to brown.

CORN STARCH PUDDING.

Warm three pints of milk, add four tablespoonfuls of corn starch, four of sugar, the yolks of six eggs, a mite of salt; put in the oven until it begins to thicken; then beat the whites and six teaspoons of sugar together; spread over it and bake until done.

CORN STARCH PUDDING, BOILED.

Take one quart of milk, place over the fire to boil; add a little salt. Take four tablespoonfuls of starch wet with cold milk; beat four eggs and add to the starch; when the milk boils, stir the starch and eggs in gradually and boil ten minutes, stirring until it is smooth; pour into a dish and serve with wine sauce. J. R. A.

PLANCHETTE PUDDING.

One quart of milk, one cup of sugar, two tablespoons of corn starch, three eggs, one cup of raisins, a little salt and vanilla. Boil the raisins soft and put them in the pudding dish; use only the yolks of the eggs for the custard; when boiled pour over the raisins; make a frosting with the whites.

CHOCOLATE PUDDING.

Scald one quart of milk; into this stir three tablespoons of grated chocolate; when cold add five eggs, saving whites of two, five tablespoons of sugar, one of corn starch dissolved in a little milk (cold), flavor to taste; bake half an hour; cover with the whites of the two eggs beaten with half a cup of brown sugar. MRS. NORRIS.

CHOCOLATE PUDDING.

One quart of milk, twelve tablespoons of grated chocolate, one-half loaf stale baker's bread, three eggs, one teaspoon of cinnamon; bake half an hour; serve with sauce.
MRS. YOUNG.

CHOCOLATE PUDDING.

One quart of milk, two eggs beaten light, three tablespoonfuls of corn starch, one-half cup of powdered sugar, one cup of grated chocolate; let the milk come to a boil; add the corn starch previously wet in a little cold milk; when this has boiled two minutes add the eggs and sugar beaten light together, and lastly add the chocolate, letting it all boil for a minute before taking off the fire. Serve cold, with sugar and cream. MRS. J. G. CHAPMAN.

DANDY PUDDING.

One quart of milk, yolks of four eggs with three tablespoonfuls corn starch, one-half cup of sugar; bring the milk to a boil and stir eggs, etc., into it; when thickened, pour into a dish and flavor with vanilla or lemon. Then add a cup of sugar to the whites of the eggs: beat them and spread over the top of the pudding, and set in the oven until a light brown. Cool the pudding before adding the meringue. Eaten cold. J. R. A.

BLACK PUDDING.

One cup of sugar, one cup of butter, one cup of milk, three tablespoonfuls of flour, three-quarters of a cup of syrup, eight eggs, one wine-glass of brandy, one nutmeg; one teaspoonful of saleratus to be put in just before baking.

Mrs. Wm. Maurice.

DANISH PUDDING.

One quart of new milk, eight eggs, half a cup of sugar. Boil the milk and pour upon the beaten yolks; beat the whites very light and stir in; take half a pound of brown sugar and burn it slightly in an iron pan, put in the bottom of an earthen pudding dish, pour the custard on top, set the dish in a pan of water, bake one hour; eat cold.

Miss E. Tucker.

FRITTERS WITHOUT MILK.

One pint of boiling water, stir in butter the size of an egg and a pint of flour, until smooth, then pour it into a deep dish; when cool enough so as not to scald the eggs, break in four eggs, only one at a time, beating it very light, then have your fat hot, dropping in a spoonful at a time.

Mrs. S. D. Glover.

SOUFFLE PUDDING.

Boil a quarter of a pound of butter in a saucepan with two tablespoonfuls of flour, stirring all the while; add a tumbler of sweet milk, stir until it becomes the consistency of starch; take from the fire and add quickly the unbeaten yolks of four eggs. Just before dinner add the whites of the eggs beaten stiff with two tablespoonfuls of white sugar, stir it through lightly and bake fifteen minutes. To be eaten with a sauce. MRS. H. C. MOORE.

GENTLEMAN'S PUDDING.

Half pound of grated cheese, quarter pound of bread crumbs, two ounces of butter, three eggs, one cup of milk. Pour over the mixed cheese, bread crumbs and butter, the warm milk with a little salt; when cool add the well beaten eggs; bake in a pudding dish, and eat hot for supper.
MRS. R. H. MORTON.

EVE'S PUDDING.

Six large sour apples chopped fine, one cup of bread crumbs, three tablespoonfuls of flour, one cup of brown sugar, one cup of currants, one small cup of butter, five eggs; mix well together, adding the eggs, well beaten, last; pour into a tin pudding mould well buttered; boil three hours; eat with sauce. MISS E. TUCKER AND MRS. WM. MAURICE.

APPLE MERINGUE.

Pare and quarter nice fair apples, stew till soft with a little water and sugar—be careful not to break them; when soft lay them in a pudding dish; for a medium sized pudding allow the whites of six eggs, beat them to a stiff froth, with a cupful of sugar, flavor with lemon; spread the eggs and sugar over the apples, and bake in the oven until it becomes a delicate brown. MRS. J. W. GODDARD.

JELLY MERINGUE PUDDING.

One pint of stale bread crumbs (baker's bread), one quart of milk, half a cup of white sugar, three eggs; the yellows of the eggs with the white of one well beaten and added to the milk and crumbs. Mix all these together and flavor with

PUDDINGS.

nutmeg or any flavor you may prefer, set it in the oven and bake slowly for two hours, take it out and let it cool, then spread over it some currant or plum jelly, take the whites of the two eggs and beat light, adding two tablespoonfuls of powdered sugar; beat till very thick, spread it over the top, and set it in the oven a minute or two until a very light brown. It must be eaten perfectly cold with cream.

E. M.

BIRDS' NEST PUDDING.

Pare the apples, leave them whole, take out the core, fill the place with sugar and lemon, put them in a square pan, make a thick batter of flour, milk and saleratus, pour upon them, and bake slowly for an hour and a half; serve with sauce. Instead of a batter of flour, etc., a nice custard may be poured over the apples, and bake half an hour.

BAKED APPLE DUMPLING PUDDING.

Make a biscuit dough, roll it out about one-half inch thick, have raw apples sliced thin, season with sugar and cinnamon spread over the middle of the dough, fold the ends of dough to the middle, dot on small pieces of butter, put into a biscuit pan with one and a half inches of water. Baste well.

SAUCE.—Thicken the water with butter and flour rubbed together, sugar and cinnamon; let it scald upon the top of the stove; if not enough water in the pan, add a little more.

MAGGIE FANNING.

BOILED APPLE DUMPLING.

Take six Irish potatoes, boil and mash them, moisten with a little milk, some salt, piece of butter size of an egg; then add flour enough to make a crust; slice the apples thin and put into the crust, after being rolled out, add a little allspice; put into a dish and steam two hours. Some prefer to have the apples whole and crust wrapped round each apple.

FRUIT PUDDING.

One quart of berries or any kind of fresh fruit mixed with one quart of flour, one tablespoonful melted butter, two teaspoonfuls of cream tartar, one teaspoonful of soda, milk enough to make a stiff batter; pour into tin pudding mould; boil in water three hours.
MRS. ROBT. CLARKE, N. Y.

WHORTLEBERRY PUDDING.

One pint of molasses and water, a tablespoon of salt, flour to make a stiff batter, one quart of berries; boil three hours. To be eaten with a cold butter and sugar sauce.
MRS. BROCK.

BLACKBERRY PUDDING.

One pound of flour, one pint of molasses, one quart of blackberries, one-half cup of milk, one teaspoon of soda, one and a half of salt, cloves, cinnamon, allspice. Boil in a mould; serve with sauce. MRS. DAN. YOUNG.

CITRON PUDDING.

One pound of sugar, the yolks of thirteen eggs well beaten, cream, nine ounces of butter; mix with the eggs and sugar; make a rich puff paste, lay it in the bottom of the dish; slice the citron thin, lay it in the bottom; pour the pudding in and bake it slowly.

GINGER PUDDING.

One cup of sugar, a quarter of a cup of butter, two eggs, half a cup of milk, one and a half cups of flour, one tablespoon of ginger, half a teaspoonful of soda.
MRS. W. H. PULSIFER.

FIG PUDDING.

Six ounces of suet, six ounces of bread crumbs, six ounces of sugar, one-half pound of figs, three eggs, one cup of milk, one-half glass of brandy, one nutmeg, two teaspoons of baking powder. Steam three hours. MRS. D. YOUNG.

PUDDINGS.

BOILED LEMON PUDDING.

One-half pound of suet, three-quarters of a pound of bread crumbs, two small lemons, six ounces of sugar, one-quarter pound of flour, two eggs and milk. Mix suet, crumbs, sugar and flour well together, adding the grated rind and juice of lemons; when well mixed moisten with the eggs and sufficient milk to make the pudding of the consistency of thick batter, put in a buttered mould, boil three and a half hours; serve with wine sauce. Mrs. D. Young.

LEMON PUDDING.

Three large tablespoonfuls of corn starch mixed with cold water very thin, add three coffee-cups of boiling water, boil till it thickens, stirring all the time, then add two coffee-cups of sugar, grated rind and juice of two large lemons, two eggs well beaten, salt to taste: butter a pudding dish and bake twenty minutes; serve cold; nice with cream.

Mrs. D. Young.

LEMON RICE PUDDING.

One teacup of rice, three pints of milk, a little salt; boil in a farina boiler three hours; pour into a pudding dish and stir into it the yolks of five eggs well beaten, a large tablespoonful of butter and one tablespoonful of sugar; beat the whites of the eggs to a stiff froth and stir in twelve tablespoonfuls of powdered sugar; grate the rind of one large lemon into the rice, and add the juice to the whites, and pour over the rice, and put into the oven until of a light brown color. Served cold. Mrs. R. H. Morton.

ORANGE PUDDING.

One pound of butter and one pound of sugar beaten to a cream, one glass of brandy, wine and rose-water mixed together, ten eggs beaten to a light froth; boil the rinds of two oranges until tender, changing the water two or three times, then beat in a mortar, add the juice with the grated rind and juice of one lemon. Mrs. D. Young.

ORANGE MARMALADE PUDDING.

One cup of fine bread crumbs, one-half cup of sugar, one cup of milk or cream, four eggs, two teaspoonfuls of butter, one cup of orange or other sweet marmalade; beat the butter and sugar together; add the yolks well beaten; then the milk, the crumbs and the whites beaten to a froth; put a layer of this in the bottom of a well buttered baking dish; then spread thickly with some thick marmalade (orange is the best); then another layer of the mixture until the dish is full, leaving the custard mixture at the top; bake in a moderate oven one hour; serve it at table with cream or custard.
E. M.

COCOANUT PUDDING.

Grate one cocoanut after having scraped off the outside skin, pound or roll fine four Boston crackers and mix with the cocoanut, add to them one quart of boiling milk and three tablespoonfuls of melted butter, or one pint of sweet cream; beat six eggs, yolks and whites separately, and stir into the mixture, add a small cup of sugar, flavor to the taste; pour into a deep dish lined with rich paste and bake about an hour; can be served warm or cold.
Mrs. E. P. Pettes.

OLD-FASHIONED BAKED RICE PUDDING.

One quart of good milk, one cup of sugar, one saltspoonful of salt, two tablespoonfuls of rice, flavor with nutmeg; bake two hours in a slow oven, and then you will have a rich creamy pudding.
E. M.

WEDDING CAKE PUDDING.

One cup of molasses, one egg, one teaspoonful of soda, one cup of milk, one cup of raisins, one cup of currants; enough flour to make a stiff batter; boil three hours in a mould.

Sauce.—Half a cup of butter creamed, with sugar, brandy and extract or nutmeg to suit taste.
Mrs. Frank A. Lane.

BOILED SALLY LUNN PUDDING.

Seven eggs, one cup of butter, two cups of sugar, two pints of flour, half a cup of yeast; make up over night, and in the morning beat in half a pound of raisins; grease a tin mould well, and put in boiling water; boil three hours; keep steady in pot; serve with sauce of sugar and butter, creamed. Mrs. F. A. Lane.

VERMICELLI PUDDING.

Wash three ounces of vermicelli, and boil till it thickens in a pint of milk, with a pinch of salt; remove it from the fire, and add three well beaten eggs, one cup of sugar, and flavor it to taste; bake half an hour; serve cold, with cream.
C. G. Hill.

APPLE FRITTERS.

One pint of milk, two eggs, a little salt, quarter of a teaspoonful of soda, half a teaspoonful of cream of tartar; make a stiff batter, stir in chopped apple, and fry like pancakes; to be eaten with sweet sauce or nice syrup.

BAKED INDIAN PUDDING.

Scald three pints of milk, and pour it on to a common-sized teacup of corn meal, add nearly a cup of molasses and a little salt; when ready for the oven, add a pint of cold milk, give it a stir round, and set it in the oven.
Mrs. Sam'l Treat.

CORN PUDDING.

To three pints of milk take two quarts of cut corn, two tablespoonfuls of flour mixed up with milk, four eggs, salt to taste; add a little butter. Bake one hour.
Mrs. Davis.

CORN PUDDING.

One-half dozen ears of corn, one-half pint of milk, three eggs well beaten, sugar and salt to taste; two tablespoons of butter, one of flour if liked; grate and scrape the corn; bake all about half an hour Mrs. E. H. Temple.

CARROT PUDDING.

Half a pound each of sugar, raisins, currants, grated raw potatoes and carrots and suet chopped fine, one pound of flour, one cup of milk, mix all together; put in a floured bag or mould; serve with a warm sauce. Boil three hours.
Mrs. D. R. Powell.

PUDDING SAUCE.

Take a piece of butter the size of an egg, nearly two tea-cups of sugar, one egg; beat all to a cream, when ready to send to table stir in a little boiling water; be sure the water is boiling, and judge the quantity by its looks—perhaps a few tablespoonfuls.
Mrs. J. T. Davis.

SAUCE.

Two cups of sugar beat with yolks of two eggs, then add the whites beaten light, then the wine for seasoning, and just before sending to the table thin with about half a cup of warm milk.
Mrs. Palmer.

PUDDING SAUCE.

One cup of sugar, one and a half tablespoonfuls of butter, two eggs, one teaspoonful of lemon; beat all up to a cream; just before taking it to the table add about a teacup of boiling water, stirring it quite fast.
Mrs. S. D. Glover.

SPLENDID PUDDING SAUCE.

One cup of sugar, one egg, pinch of salt; beat together twenty minutes, just before wanted boil a little over a tea-cup of milk, add flavoring of wine or brandy, pour the boiling milk on to the sugar and egg, stir all together quickly.
Mrs. Damon, New York.

AUNT MARY'S SAUCE.

Two eggs, beat yolks and whites separately, one and a half cupfuls of sugar, two tablespoonfuls of butter, one gill of milk; stir all well together, and cook same as float. This is splendid sauce for apple dumplings.

SAUCE.

Add to one coffee-cup of boiling milk one tablespoonful of flour wet with two of cold milk; have ready one teacup of sugar and one-half teacup of butter stirred together, and when the milk and flour have boiled two or three minutes add the sugar and butter; stir well, but do not boil; flavor with vanilla.

HARD PUDDING SAUCE.

Two and a half cups of sugar, one cup of butter, brandy; beat well together. Mrs. Wm. Maurice.

PIES.

EXTRA NICE.

Pastry for seven pies, three uncovered. Three pints of flour, one pound of butter and a heaping cup of lard; wash the butter in ice-water to extract the salt: set the pan in which you mix the pastry in one filled with ice-water; mix very lightly with ice water, the flour and lard and one cup of the butter; roll the paste thin three times, always rolling from you, and each time adding one-third the butter, in small pieces, and dredging in flour. Set it on ice and let it harden before using. MRS. KRUM.

PASTRY.

Mix one-third of a pound of butter with one and a half pounds of sifted flour, using ice-water enough to moisten it; roll it out into a thin sheet, always rolling from you quickly and lightly. Cut two-thirds of a pound of butter into small bits, and when the paste is thin enough take one third of them and stick in close rows upon the sheet; dredge with flour; roll up the paste into close folds as you would a sheet of music; flatten it and roll out as before, adding another third of the bits of butter; do this three times. Finally cut off from the end of the roll a piece large enough to cover a pie plate and roll out quickly; butter your pie plates and fit the paste neatly in them; gather up the scraps and use in the next sheet. If a top crust is needed lay the paste on, cut to fit, and press down the edges with a knife or spoon, ornamenting it in regular form. Bake until a light brown. When the time can be spared it improves the pie crust, after all the butter has been used up, to lay the roll on ice for a quarter of an hour or more. MARY COLBURT.

CHOP PASTRY.

Six cups of flour, two cups of shortening, two cups of water, salt; chop well until it mixes; it need not be touched with the hands until it is ready to roll.

MINCE MEAT.

Two pounds of meat after being boiled, four pounds of apples, one pound of suet, two pounds of sugar, one and a half pounds of raisins, one-half pint of molasses, one-half pint of brandy, one-half pint of wine, one quart of cider, four tablespoonfuls of salt, one of cinnamon, one teaspoonful of cloves, one tablespoonful of essence of lemon, one tablespoonful of mace, two nutmegs.

MINCE PIES.

Two pounds chopped meat (save the water it is boiled in), four pounds of apples (Belleflower), eight nutmegs, two pounds of raisins, two pounds of currants, one pound of citron, half a teacup of cinnamon, two teaspoonfuls of cloves, two teaspoonfuls of mace, one pint of molasses, three or four pounds of sugar, three or four tablespoonfuls of salt, one pound of beef suet chopped fine, cider and wine, or brandy.

Mrs. T. T. Richards and Mrs. W. H. Pulsifer.

SUMMER MINCE PIES.

Five soda crackers, roll them fine, and pour over them two cups of boiling water; add one cup of molasses, half a cup of vinegar, one cup of raisins, one cup of currants, half a cup of melted butter, half a cup of brandy, one grated lemon and juice, salt, cloves, cinnamon. This will make four good sized pies. Mrs. Wm. Maurice.

COCOANUT PIE.

Four ounces of butter and one pound of sugar beaten together, nine eggs, twelve ounces of grated cocoanut, one tumbler of cream, one gill of rose-water.

Mrs. R. H. Morton.

COCOANUT PIE.

One and a half cups of sugar, one and a half cups of milk, one tablespoonful of butter, the rind of one lemon, and one cocoanut finely grated. MRS. KLINE.

RAISIN PIES.

One cup of sugar, one cup of raisins, one egg, one cracker soaked in milk, juice of one lemon, and the rind chopped fine. To be baked in tarts or turnovers.

MUSH PIES.

Four eggs, one teacup of sugar, two tablespoonfuls of mush, two tablespoonfuls of butter, one teaspoonful of extract of lemon; bake as custard pies. MRS. WELLS.

TRANSPARENT PIES.

For two pies—four eggs, two cups of sugar; beat eggs and sugar together; little over half a teacup of butter, melt the butter if the weather is cold and pour into the eggs and sugar, three tablespoonfuls of sweet milk, flavor with lemon; make a bottom crust, put the custard in and bake.

MRS. T. J. ALBRIGHT, Kirkwood.

CUSTARD PIE.

One quart of milk, five eggs, take out the whites, beat the eggs, add one-half cup of sugar, a little salt, flavor to suit; fill the pans and bake. While the pies are baking beat the whites of the eggs to a froth, add one spoonful of white sugar, beat again, and when the pies are baked spread the frosting on top, put them in the oven and brown.

MRS. LEWIS E. KLINE.

CREAM PIE.

Take as much thick sweet cream as will fill a pie plate, add whites of two eggs beaten to a froth, sugar enough to taste, flavor with lemon; bake as custard.

MRS. POWELL.

VERY FINE CREAM PIE.

Half a pound of butter, four eggs, sugar to taste, a little salt, nutmeg to taste, two tablespoons of arrowroot, pour on it a quart of boiling milk, stir the whole together; bake as custard. MRS. POWELL.

LEMON PIES.

The grated peel and juice of three lemons, three cups of crushed white sugar, yolks of four eggs beaten well, then add the peel and juice, stir until light, then bake; after baking, beat up the whites stiff with sugar, and spread over the pies, then place in the oven to brown.
. MRS. G. F. FILLEY.

LEMON PIES.

(TWO PIES.)

Three lemons, three cups of sugar, five eggs, a piece of butter the size of an egg; beat the yolks, lemon, sugar and butter together, then two small cups of milk and one tablespoonful of corn starch, add the whites beaten light; bake in puff paste with one crust. MRS. S. R. FILLEY.

SPLENDID LEMON PIES.

Six eggs, two lemons if juicy, three if dry, one pint of sugar, one-half pint of butter; mix yolks of eggs, butter and sugar together, add one tablespoonful of sifted flour; beat very light, put in lemon and white of egg beat to a stiff froth; bake as custard in puff paste with one crust.

LEMON PIES.

(THREE PIES.)

Grate the rind of three lemons, beat to a cream the yolks of seven eggs, add a tablespoon of flour to each pie, a small piece of butter, sugar to taste, put in the juice, then gradually pour in three teacups of water; beat the whites to a froth and apply after baking. MISS LOUISE VOGT.

LEMON PIES.

Grated rind and juice of three large lemons, ten eggs, yolks and whites beaten separately, one cup of bread crumbs grated, half pint of melted butter, three or four cups of sugar, according to taste. Beat the yolks of the eggs, and to these add all the ingredients, the whites stirred in last: they should be put into the pies and baked as quickly as possible. MRS. F. G. GODDARD.

LEMON PIE.

Cream, one tablespoonful of butter, seven tablespoonfuls of sugar, six eggs, leaving out the whites of four, a tumbler of sweet milk, the grated rind and juice of two large lemons. While the pies are baking, make a meringue of four whites of eggs and four tablespoonfuls of sugar: put in the oven and brown. MISS SEMPLE.

LEMON CHEESE CAKES.

One pound of loaf sugar, one-quarter pound of butter, yolks of six eggs, whites of four, juice of three lemons, grated rind of two. Put all in a pan, simmer over a clear fire till it becomes thick like honey, stir it one way; make a nice paste, line patty-pans, put in some of the above, and bake in a moderately quick oven.

GOLDEN PIE.

One cup of sugar, one cup of new milk, one tablespoonful of corn starch, yolks of three eggs well beaten, juice and peel of one lemon. Pour into a rich paste; when baked add the whites of eggs beaten with three tablespoonfuls of sugar, and brown. MRS. D. YOUNG.

ORANGE PIE.

Grate the peel of one fresh orange and take the juice and pulp of two, add to them one teacup of sugar and the beaten yolks of three eggs; mix one cup of milk with the whites of the eggs beaten to a stiff froth; bake in puff paste. This rule makes one pie. MRS. E. P. PETTES.

PEACH PIE.

Line a pie plate with good paste, and lay in the fruit peeled, stoned and sliced, sprinkling sugar over them in proportion to their sweetness; chop three peach kernels fine for every pie; pour in a little water, and bake with an upper crust.

PEACH COBBLER.

Take a deep dish, line with paste, put an inverted teacup in the center of the dish, fill with whole peaches, pared, packing them well, and sweetening to taste, water almost enough to fill the dish; cover with crust and bake.

Miss E. L. Glover.

CRANBERRY TART.

Stew until soft in a saucepan, with enough water to cover them, the cranberries well washed and looked over, run through a cullender to remove the skins, and sweeten to taste; bake in pastry shells, with a cross-bar of pastry over the top.

CELEBRATED RHUBARB PIE.

For one large pie, or three small deep ones. Take the stalks, cut off the leaves, and rinse in cold water (do not strip off the skin, as it contains much of the flavor), cut in half-inch lengths, and add from one to three teacups of sugar, according to the acidity of the rhubarb; stir in a large bowl, so that the materials may be well mixed; add one lemon cut up very fine, peel and all the juice well squeezed in, one nutmeg, grated, one tablespoonful of essence of lemon, one good pinch of salt, one tablespoonful of sifted flour, two tablespoonfuls of butter; make a nice crust, and bake from a half to three-quarters of an hour; make a slit in the top of your pie, and bake in a deep pan, so that its chief excellence shall not waste by boiling over.

RHUBARB TART.

One pint of stewed pie-plant, four ounces of sugar, half a pint of cream, two ounces of crackers, three eggs.

SWEET POTATO PIE.

One quart of sweet potatoes boiled and well strained through a sieve, three beaten eggs, three tablespoonfuls of sugar, three tablespoonfuls of butter, one and a half grated nutmegs, one-half teaspoonful of ground cinnamon, a less quantity of ground cloves, a little lemon peel or essence of lemon, enough cream to make the mixture a thin batter. Make a rich paste, and, covering your baking-plates, pour in the mixture and bake without a top paste.

MRS. LEWIS E. KLINE.

SWEET POTATO PIE.

Half a pound of potatoes boiled and mashed, half a pound of sugar, half a pound of butter, eight eggs, if you make a meringue, six if not, stir to a cream the sugar and butter, add potatoes, then yolks of eggs beaten, then whites of four eggs, meringue with the rest; flavor with nutmeg and lemon.

MRS. BALLENTINE.

APPLE CUSTARD PIE.

Stew the apples and strain through a cullender, add two eggs, half a cup of milk, a small piece of butter, and flavor with lemon and sugar to taste. If you wish it nice, leave out the whites of the eggs and make a meringue.

MRS. MICHAEL.

APPLE SLUMP.

Pare and slice thin two quarts of apples, put in a porcelain kettle with a cup of molasses, a cup of sugar, one teaspoonful of cinnamon, half a cup of water. Make a crust of one pint of flour, a tablespoonful of lard, a little salt, two teaspoonfuls of yeast powder, mix with a little water; roll your dough out the size of your kettle, lay it over the apples, cutting a slit in the centre, cover over with a tight lid to keep the steam in, cook for an hour; when done, lift the crust off on to a plate and pour the apples on it.

MRS. CHAS. FREEBORN.

APPLE DOWDY.

Pare and slice apples very thin, put them in a tin pan with half a cup of water, make a crust same as for pies, roll it out and lay it over the apples, pressing it down all round the edge, put into the oven and bake. When done, take off the crust, break it up in pieces about two inches square, then sweeten the apples, add half a teaspoonful of cinnamon, a little more water, pour over the crust, mix all together, let stand until they get cold; serve with cream.

CONNECTICUT APPLE PIE.

Take tart winter apples; pare, core and slice them; line the pie plates with a good crust; fill with the apples, adding a little water, put on the top cover and bake. When baked, take off the cover; season with sugar, a little cinnamon and bits of butter; replace the cover; sprinkle with sugar and serve. Mrs. O. D. Filley.

APPLE PIE.

Six apples grated, two eggs, two cups of sugar, two lemons squeezed and grated; put on the stove to thicken, and if it does not, stir in a little corn starch; fill the pie plates lined with crust, and bake.
Mrs. James Bartlett.

SPICED APPLE TARTS.

Rub stewed or baked apples through a sieve; sweeten them and add powdered mace and cinnamon sufficient to flavor them; squeeze the juice of a lemon in and grate the peel; line the patty-pans with a light crust, and bake.
Mrs. Lewis E. Kline.

MOCK PUMKIN PIE.

Four large grated apples, two eggs, a little butter and sugar; flavor with lemon; fill the crust and bake; then spread over the top of the pie a thick meringue made by beating to a stiff froth the whites of three eggs for each pie, sweetened with three tablespoons of sugar and flavored with rose-water, vanilla or lemon; put in the oven until lightly browned. Saratoga.

PUMPKIN PIE.

One quart of pumpkin stewed and strained, six eggs, the whites and yolks beaten separately, one quart of milk, one teaspoonful of cinnamon, one teaspoonful of nutmeg, one cup and a half of white sugar; flavor with two tablespoonfuls of wine or brandy; beat all well together, and bake in crust without cover. Make squash pie in the same way.   MISS E. L. GLOVER.

CHERRY PIE.

Line the dish with a good crust, and fill with ripe cherries, stoned or not, as preferred, dredge flour over the top, and sprinkle sugar enough to sweeten them, rub the edge of the pie crust with cold water, put a top cover on, with a slit in the centre to prevent boiling over, and bake; sift white sugar over the top before serving. Blackberry, raspberry and plum pies are made in the same way.

GREEN GOOSEBERRY TART.

Look over the gooseberries, and stew slowly, with enough water over them to keep from burning, until they break, sweeten well and put aside to cool; pour into pastry shells, and bake with a top crust of puff paste; brush all over with beaten egg while hot; put in the oven for three minutes to glaze.

CURRANT AND RASPBERRY TART.

Allow a third more currants than raspberries; mix well together, sweeten, and fill the crust, put top cover on and bake; sift white sugar over the top, and serve while warm.

NICE DESSERTS.

LEMON BUTTER.

One pound of pulverized white sugar, the whites of six eggs and yolks of two, together with three lemons, including grated rind and juice; cook it over a slow fire for twenty minutes, stirring it constantly.
Mrs. Lewis E. Kline.

HEDGE-HOG.

Take two pounds of blanched almonds, beat them with a little rose-water, beat in the yolks of twelve eggs and the whites of seven, half a pint of sweetened cream, quarter pound of the best butter creamed; set it over a slow fire until it gets quite stiff, then make it in the form of a hedgehog, stick it over with blanched almonds; cut in thin pieces; you can set it on wine jelly.
Mrs. D. Young.

SNOW PUDDING.

Soak half a box of Nelson's gelatine in a teacup of cold water half an hour or longer, pour on it one pint of boiling water; strain when dissolved and put in a cool place, but do not let it harden; take the whites of three eggs, beat these, adding by degrees three teacups of white sugar and the juice of two lemons; when thoroughly mixed and light, add by degrees the cool gelatine beaten until light as snow, perfectly even and somewhat stiff; put in moulds to harden; when ready for use, place in a dish and pour around it a nice delicate custard.
Mrs. R. H. Morton.

CREAM SNOW.

One teacup of sweet cream, one teacup of sugar, two eggs, one teaspoonful of corn starch; melt the cream and sugar together and dissolve the starch; when cool stir in the eggs and also snow until quite stiff.

ITALIAN SNOW.

Half a box of Cox's gelatine to one pint of cold water, whites of three eggs, one cup of sugar, flavoring of any kind of extract, beat with egg-beater for twenty minutes, pour into moulds, thoroughly dissolve the gelatine before adding the eggs. To be eaten with cream.

Mrs. E. J. Clark, Carondelet.

APPLE SNOW.

Put twelve tart apples in cold water and set them over a slow fire; when soft drain off the water, strip off the skins, core, and lay them in a deep dish; beat the whites of twelve eggs to a froth, put in half a pound of powdered sugar to the apples, beat to a stiff froth, and add the beaten eggs; beat the whole to a stiff snow, turn into a dessert dish, and ornament with myrtle or box.

APPLE FLOAT.

Sweeten and season with mace or nutmeg, a small bowl of apple sauce (which has been through a sieve); then add the whites of three eggs beaten to a stiff froth. Eat with cream and sugar.

Mrs. R. H. Morton.

ORANGE SOUFFLE.

Peel and slice three oranges, one pint of milk, yolks of five eggs; sweeten to taste. When done pour on oranges; beat the whites to a froth; pour gently over oranges; put in oven and brown.

Mrs. Sarah Davis.

OMELET SOUFFLE.

One cup of flour, one pint of milk, one spoonful of sugar, butter size of a walnut, scald milk, flour and butter together; after the batter is cold stir in the yolks of five eggs; stir in the whites of the eggs well beaten just before baking. Bake in a quick oven; eat with sauce. This is a splendid pudding.

Miss E. H. Glover.

OMELET SOUFFLE.

Beat the whites of three eggs; when beaten up light add one tablespoonful of marmalade or the juice of fresh fruit of any kind; mix this spoonful of flavoring with one cup of powdered sugar, and turn well for one-fourth of an hour. Rub on earthen pudding dish with butter; turn the omelet into it and bake a light brown in a very quick oven. Serve immediately.   Mrs. J. G. Chapman.

SNOW PUDDING.

One pint of boiling water poured on one-half box of gelatine, put in the juice of two lemons and two cups of sugar; beat the whites of four eggs to a solid froth and stir into the mixture, and set it away to cool. Take the four yolks of the eggs and sweeten to taste; boil one and a half pints of milk and pour in the eggs while boiling, as for soft custards; flavor as you please and set away to cool. The white part will be the pudding; the custard will serve as the sauce; it is better to make this the day before, so it will be very cold.

Mrs. Richards, Mrs. H. C. Moore and others.

BOILED CUSTARD.

Three eggs, one pint of milk, one cup of sugar; scald the milk and pour it on the eggs and sugar, which should be well beaten together; pour it into a kettle, place it over the fire, and stir until thick and creamy.

Mrs. Lewis E. Kline.

COFFEE CUSTARD.

Three tablespoonfuls of sugar, yolks of four eggs, mix; add half a pint of milk, one cup of strong coffee; when mixed boil ten minutes, then bake; frost with the whites of eggs.   Mrs. D. Young.

TAPIOCA CUSTARD.

Three-quarters of a teacup of tapioca, three-quarters of a teacup of white sugar, one quart of rich milk, two eggs and flavoring; soak the tapioca in the milk three hours, keeping it in a warm place; when ready to make, put it in a porcelain kettle, which set in another kettle of hot water, put over the fire and heat slowly, heating it until it is quite melted; beat well the eggs and sugar, stirring into the milk when it is scalding hot; continue stirring constantly until the mixture is quite smooth and thick (do not let it boil), then pour into a pudding dish, spread over the top the whites, which have been previously whipped and sweetened with a little sugar; set in a quick oven, brown the top and take out as quickly as possible.

This dish requires some experience to make it just right; although the whites make a prettier appearance on top. I think the custard tastes nicer to beat them in with the yolks; then, of course, it is not necessary to put it in the oven.

MRS. W. FALLON.

ALMOND CUSTARD.

One-quarter of a pound of almonds blanched and beaten with a little rose-water, one pint of cream, yolks of four eggs; mix all together, put over a slow fire until it thickens; keep it well stirred; serve in dishes or glasses.

MRS. D. YOUNG.

CREAM CHANTILLY.

One ounce of American isinglass dissolved in a small pint of milk sweetened and flavored to taste; beat one and a half pints of cream to a froth, mix with the dissolved isinglass; when cold, but not hard, beat all hard together until light; Madeira wine and vanilla make the nicest flavoring. If you use wine, put it in when you beat all together. The cream beats much easier and lighter for being cold. It must be very sweet, as you have to add the cream afterwards.
MRS. R. H. MORTON.

FINE BLANC MANGE.

One quart of cream, half a pound of lump sugar, half a pint of wine, half paper of gelatine, juice and peel of lemon,

Mix half of the cream and all the sugar thoroughly, put in the lemon, then the wine, the gelatine dissolved in the rest of the cream thoroughly.   MRS. E. F. RICHARDS.

SPANISH BLANC MANGE.

Half a pound of sugar, one lemon, juice and rind, mix with one pint of cream and half a pint of wine; stir the mixture till all the articles are thoroughly mixed, then stir in gradually a second pint of cream; dissolve one ounce of gelatine in hot water, and when it becomes lukewarm add it gradually to the mixture.

CHOCOLATE BLANC MANGE.

One ounce of gelatine dissolved in as much water as will cover it (about two-thirds of a pint), four ounces of chocolate grated, one quart of milk, three-quarters of a pound of sugar. Boil the sugar, milk and chocolate together five minutes, put in the gelatine, and let the whole boil five minutes more, stirring to prevent burning; add a teaspoonful of vanilla extract, and put in moulds to cool. It should be made the day before it is needed.   MRS. BROCK.

CHOCOLATE BLANC MANGE.

Take one quart of milk, four tablespoonfuls of corn starch, a pinch of salt, three tablespoonfuls of sugar, and two squares of grated chocolate. Take from the quart of milk one teacup of the cold milk to mix with the chocolate; to the rest of the cold milk add the sugar, chocolate and salt, let it come to a good boil; mix the corn starch with a little milk, one teaspoonful of vanilla, then add that to the boiling milk, stir it until it thickens, pour into moulds; eat with cream.   MRS. E. J. CLARK.

AMBROSIA.

Peel and slice your oranges thin; make a layer of oranges, sprinkle with sugar, then a layer of grated cocoanut; or some prefer to have the grated cocoanut served in a dish by itself, and sprinkled over the oranges as you serve them out.

ICED APPLES.

Pare and core one dozen large apples, fill with sugar, very little butter, cinnamon; bake till nearly done, let them cool, pour off the juice, put icing on the top and sides, set in the oven a minute or two and brown slightly; serve with cream.

Mrs. Lewis E. Kline.

CHARLOTTE RUSSE.

Line the pan with lady-fingers (or nice light cake of any kind), take a quart of cream, sweeten to taste, and flavor with essence of vanilla, then whip it; pour a cup of hot water on half an ounce of gelatine; after it is dissolved stir very hard into the whipped cream, then pour into the mould carefully, not to upset the cake.

CHARLOTTE RUSSE.

One quart of milk, one pint of cream, six eggs, sugar, wine and vanilla to taste, one ounce of gelatine put in the cream and placed on the stove to dissolve; make a custard of milk and yolks of the eggs, pour it while hot over the whites previously beaten to a stiff froth, stir in the cream and flavor, let it stand awhile to cool; line your mould with sponge or any light cake cut thin, and pour in the mixture slowly so as not to displace the cake.

CHARLOTTE RUSSE.

Extract the flavor of a vanilla bean by boiling it in a half a pint of milk, then strain the milk, and when cold add one-quarter of a pound of loaf sugar, beat the yolks of four eggs very light and stir them into the mixture, heat it over the fire for five minutes until it becomes a custard, but be careful that it does not boil; boil an ounce of isinglass with a pint of water, and be sure it is thoroughly dissolved before using it, and one-half of the water boiled away. The custard being cold, drain the isinglass into it and stir them hard together; leave them to cool while you prepare the rest of the mixture; whip a quart of rich cream to a froth and mix it with the custard; the safest way to whip cream light is to remove the froth with a strainer as fast as it gathers, until the whole is whipped; lay a piece of white paper the size of the mould in the bottom, then line the sides with lady-fingers or other sponge-cake, pour in the custard, cover over with a piece of white paper, and set it on ice mixed with coarse salt. It should set at least three or four hours.

Mrs. Frank Filley.

TO MAKE WHIPS.

Take two pints of rich cream, add one wine-glass of brandy, one wine-glass of sherry, the juice of one lemon, one cup of white sugar; beat the cream to a stiff froth with a whip-churn; have ready twelve whip-glasses filled nearly a third full of strawberry preserve, then put the whipped cream on top.

Mrs. G. Leighton.

LEMON CREAMS.

Put the juice and rind of two lemons into one pint of water, beat six eggs, and add to the water half a pound of sugar, strain through a fine sieve, and keep over the fire till as thick as custard.

Mrs. Wentworth.

ALMOND CUSTARDS.

Quarter pound of almonds blanched and pounded fine, one pint of cream, quarter pound of sugar, yolks of four eggs, two tablespoonfuls of rose-water. Stir this over the fire till thick.

Mrs. Wentworth.

ENGLISH CREAM.

One ounce of shred isinglass, three pints of milk, five eggs; sweeten and flavor to taste; eggs not cooked in.

Mrs. R. H. Morton.

VELVET CREAM.

Dissolve one ounce of gelatine in a tumbler of wine, add the peel and juice of one lemon, two cups of sugar to one quart of cream; pour in a mould.

VELVET CREAM.

One ounce of gelatine dissolved in one pint of milk, put on the fire and stir until dissolved, the yolks of two eggs beaten and stirred in while hot, make very sweet, and flavor with vanilla; when cold, but not set, add one pint of cream beaten to a froth, and the whites of two eggs beaten to a froth and flavored with wine; beat very hard.
MRS. R. H. MORTON.

VELVET CREAM.

Three sheets of isinglass, half a cup of wine, half a cup of cold water, one cup of sugar, one pint of cream, one teaspoonful of vanilla; pour the water upon the isinglass until it is dissolved, set it on the stove, then strain into the moulds.
MRS. W. MAURICE.

ITALIAN CREAM.

Take three pints of cream or milk, sweeten with white sugar, flavor with lemon or vanilla, add one ounce of isinglass, stir constantly until it boils, beat up well the yolks of eight eggs, stir them into the boiling milk, strain into mould, and let it stand upon ice five or six hours; serve with sugar and cream.
MRS. R. H. MORTON.

SPANISH CREAM.

One quart of milk, half a box of gelatine; dissolve the gelatine in the milk half an hour or more, set it on the fire until thoroughly dissolved, pour into it the yolks of four eggs well beaten and three tablespoonfuls of powdered sugar; let it stand on the stove until it thickens, stirring all the time, but do not let it boil; take it off and pour in the whites of the four eggs and three tablespoonfuls of powdered sugar well beaten, stir all together quickly, add one teaspoonful of extract of lemon.
MRS. ELLIS.

SPANISH CREAM.

Dissolve two-thirds of a box of Cox's gelatine in a quart of milk, boil twenty minutes in a tin vessel set in hot water, beat the yolks of eight eggs with a coffee-cup of sugar until quite light, take off the boiling milk and stir in rapidly the yolks and sugar, place in the hot water again and cook a few minutes, taking care that it does not curdle; beat the whites of the eggs to a stiff froth, put them in a large bowl, and pour the mixture on them slowly, stirring quickly; mix well, flavor and put in moulds.

ISABELLA CREAM.

Quarter of a box of gelatine, one pint of milk, three eggs; with the eggs and milk make a boiled custard; dissolve the gelatine in a little extra milk and add to the custard after it cools; flavor with vanilla and sweeten to taste, then whip one pint of cream and add to it, also one wine-glass of wine; set to cool.

ORANGE CREAM.

Pare the rind of an orange very thin and squeeze the juice of four oranges, and put it with peel into a pan with one pint of water, four ounces of sugar, and the whites of five eggs well beaten; mix all together, place it over a slow fire, stir in one direction until it looks thick and white, strain it through a gauze sieve, and stir it until cold.

MRS. LEWIS E. KLINE.

TAPIOCA CREAM.

Five tablespoonfuls of tapioca soaked in a pint of water over night; in the morning add the yolks of four eggs, one cup of sugar, a little salt and lemon or vanilla, one quart of milk, and boil as you would soft custard; beat the whites to a stiff froth, put them into a pudding-dish, and pour over the boiling liquid; can be eaten either cold or hot.

MRS. W. MAURICE.

CHOCOLATE GELATINE.

Dissolve one square of chocolate in a quarter of a cup of boiling water, two tablespoonfuls of gelatine in one and a half cups of cold water, two-thirds of a cup of sugar,

RICE CREAM.

One teacup of rice boiled in milk until quite soft, sweeten with white sugar, pour it into a dish, put lumps of jelly or preserved fruit on it, beat the whites of three eggs very light, half a cup of sugar, flavor with lemon; to this add about a tablespoonful of rich cream, and pour it over the rice and jelly.

CHARLOTTE POLONAISE.

Make a custard of one quart of cream, four eggs, sweeten it; pound half a pound of citron to a paste in a mortar, pound half a pound of macaroons pulverized, mix this with one-half the custard; grate half a pound of chocolate, mix with the other half of the custard; thicken both with one-quarter box of gelatine; cut a sponge cake in layers, and spread a layer of these mixtures alternately over the top. The custard should be cool enough to be still.

COCOANUT PUFFS.

Mix two cups of grated cocoanut with one cup of powdered sugar, the beaten whites of two eggs, and two tablespoonfuls of flour or corn starch; shape in little pyramids, put on buttered tins, and bake quick.

MRS. E. F. RICHARDS.

CHOCOLATE PUFFS.

Beat stiff the whites of three eggs, beat in gradually half a pound of sugar (scant), grate two ounces of chocolate, dredge it with flour, mixing in the flour well, add this gradually to the eggs and sugar, stir the whole very hard; cover the bottom of the pan with white paper, place on it thin spots of powdered sugar the size of a half-dollar, pile a portion of the mixture in each, smoothing with a knife, sift a little sugar over each; bake in a quick oven a few minutes; loosen from the paper with a broad knife.

MRS. D. YOUNG.

LEMON CREAM.

One pint of thick cream, yolks of two eggs well beaten, one cup of white sugar, rind of one lemon grated; boil and stir till nearly cold; drop a piece of lemon in a dish, and pour the cream upon it. MRS. G. F. FILLEY.

SPANISH CREAM.

Three pints of milk, one ounce of Cooper's isinglass, six eggs, six tablespoonfuls of sugar; beat up the isinglass into the milk and put over the fire to heat very slowly; beat the yolks of the eggs with the sugar and stir in when the isinglass is dissolved and the milk nearly boiling; let it thicken but not curdle, and remove it from the fire; stir in very hard the whites of the eggs beaten to a froth, flavor to taste (vanilla is best), and pour immediately into a mould or pan and set in a cold place. It must be made five or six hours before wanted, so as to turn out nicely. Eat with cream.
MRS. FOOTE, Erie.

FLUMMERY.

Put five or six slices of stale sponge jelly or any other light cake in a glass bowl; season the cake with a little wine, then pour over it a nice boiled custard made of one quart of milk and yolks of four eggs; beat the whites up very light and a little powdered sugar with them; put over the custard, piling up prettily, and add dashes of currant or any red jelly. MRS. E. F. RICHARDS.

APPLES WITH RICE.

Half a pound of rice clear, one quart of fresh milk two ounces of fresh butter, quarter of a pound of sugar; boil together till rice is soft; yolks of six eggs, mix with rice, beat whites with half a pound of sugar and mix; core twelve or fourteen apples and stew with a little butter and a small piece of stick cinnamon, a bit of lemon-peel to flavor; put the mixture into china bakers, and bake in a hot oven.
REVERE HOUSE.

ORANGE PUDDING.

Slice your oranges and sweeten to taste, catching the juice to put in the custard; lay these oranges around a glass bowl, then make a custard of three eggs to one pint of milk and a little gelatine; pour it when cold over the oranges: afterwards beat the whites of several eggs to a froth and lay on the top. MRS. WM. E. WARE.

OMELET SOUFFLE.

Five eggs to one cup of sugar, beat yolks and sugar together ten minutes, before baking add the juice of one lemon; beat the whites to a stiff froth, stir all together gently, bake in a quick oven.

MRS. GEO. W. BLAGDEN, Boston.

CARAMEL CUSTARD.

Make a custard of six eggs to one quart of milk, sugar to taste, flavor with vanilla or lemon, boil the milk, put into a round or oval tin four or five tablespoonfuls of light brown sugar, setting it on the range to melt, stirring it all the while till soft, or can be rubbed around the pan with the spoon, set this pan in a dripping-pan, with hot water half the depth of pan, pour into the sugar the custard, put into the oven and bake till firm, or you can run a knife in and it comes out clean; let it get cold; just before dinner run a knife around the custard and turn it out on a platter; it must be done carefully and quickly so as not to break, as it should be whole and firm.

MRS. EZRA FARNSWORTH, Boston.

FRIARS OMELET.

Boil or stew twelve apples, as for sauce, stir in one-quarter of a pound of butter, quarter of a pound of sugar; when cold, add four eggs well beaten, a little lemon juice; put the whole in a form of white ware; the form or dish must be buttered, and crumbs of bread thickly strewn over the bottom and sides. After the mixture is in, the top must be plentifully strewn with crumbs when baked, turn it out as blanc mange, and grate sugar over it.

MRS. SAM'L TREAT.

CONFECTIONERY.

CANDY.

Three cups of A sugar, one cup of water, two tablespoonfuls of vinegar, butter one-half the size of an egg; boil without stirring; add essence, and pull as quickly as possible. MRS. LEWIS E. KLINE.

PRAULEENS.

Take enough milk to moisten two pounds of brown sugar, (about one-half a cup); when nearly boiled put in a tablespoon of vinegar, then stir in the nuts until it sugars.
MRS. WALTER DONNELL.

SUGAR CANDY.

Three pints of clarified sugar, one-half cup of milk, one-half cup of vinegar, a piece of butter the size of an egg.

CREAM CANDY.

Two cups of white granulated sugar wet with one-half cup of vinegar, one-half cup of water; when boiling, add one tablespoon of butter; when nearly done put in vanilla; take off when it strings from the spoon, and pull while hot; must not stir or it will sugar. MRS. JAMES BARTLETT.

WHITE CREAM CANDY.

To a pint of sugar add a teacup of warm water, one tablespoonful of vinegar, flavor with vanilla; boil till hard, and try in cold water: then let cool, and pull until white.
MISS NANNIE ORRICK.

CARAMELS.

One cup of sugar, one cup of milk, two cups of molasses, one cup of grated chocolate, piece of butter size of an egg.
Mrs. J. W. Goddard.

SUGAR CANDY.

Three pints of sugar, half a cup of milk, half a cup of vinegar, and a piece of butter half the size of an egg; put the ingredients in a kettle and boil, stirring it as little as possible, until it congeals on dropping into cold water; turn into shallow pans, cool, and pull it until white. Cut in small pieces and lay on a buttered dish.
Miss M. Krum.

TAFFY CANDY.

One pound of crushed sugar, one cup of water, one teaspoonful of cream of tartar, a little vanilla; when well boiled together pour on marble or a cold plate, and pull.
Mrs. H. McKittrick.

CHOCOLATE CARAMELS.

One cup of molasses, two cups of brown sugar; boil a few moments, add one cup of milk, one and a half cups of chocolate, beaten together, one large teaspoonful of vanilla and a small piece of butter.
Mrs. Brock.

CARAMELS.

One cake of Baker's chocolate, one pint of milk, six ounces of butter, three pounds of sugar, two and a half tablespoonfuls of extract of vanilla; grate the chocolate, and mix smooth with the milk, then add the sugar and butter, and boil until it hardens when dropped in cold water. Just before taking from the fire, add the vanilla, pouring into shallow pans to cool, and just before hard, mark with a knife in small squares.
Miss M. Krum.

PEPPERMINTS.

Two cups of sugar, one-half cup of water, boil eight minutes, beat to a stiff froth, add one teaspoonful of peppermint, drop on tins.
Mrs. J. W. Goddard.

ICE-CREAM CANDY.

Three cups of sugar, crushed or cut loaf, little less than half a cup of vinegar, one and a half cups of water, a piece of butter the size of a walnut, flavor with vanilla, work it.
Mrs. J. W. Goddard.

CREAM CHOCOLATES.

Take half a pound of Baker's chocolate, cut into small pieces and put into a bowl over the tea-kettle to melt; mix five cups of sifted sugar with one cup of water and boil hard five minutes, stir into it a tablespoonful of extract of vanilla, take it off the fire and stir quickly till it begins to be white and hard, then roll into little balls and put them on a greased pan, and when perfectly hard they must be covered with the chocolate and put in a cool place to dry.
Mrs. Hugh Campbell.

MISS FLETCHER'S CANDY.

Two pounds of coffee-sugar, one cup of cold water, two tablespoonfuls of butter, one tablespoonful of vinegar, two tablespoonfuls of extract; don't stir after it is dissolved; boil according to judgment—about fifteen minutes to every two pounds.

FRENCH KISSES.

The whites of two eggs beaten very stiff, six heaping tablespoonfuls of pulverized sugar beaten into the eggs until too stiff to run; flavor; have ready some greased paper, put upon a board, and then drop some of the egg and sugar in egg-shape on the paper, set in the oven to brown lightly; then take a knife and slip your kisses from the paper, and put two together while hot.

CAKES.

In making cake always use the best butter and sugar. For ordinary cake use powdered sugar; for sponge cake some prefer the pulverized, others the granulated; and for fruit cake brown sugar, not too moist, as it will be heavy; for this cake it is also nicer to brown the flour by spreading on a biscuit pan and putting in the oven. The ordinary method of mixing cake is to first cream the butter and sugar by putting them in a bowl and thoroughly mixing with a wooden spoon, or some prefer the hand, the warmth of the hand quickening the process. Then take part of the milk and part of the flour alternately; if you use soda and cream tartar, dissolve your soda in the milk and sift the cream tartar in the flour. Then break each egg over a teacup to see if good, before mixing together; beat the yolks light and mix with the cake dough; then beat the whites to a stiff froth, and add lastly the flavor, and it is ready for the pans, which should be well greased with lard. Always have the flour well sifted. If you use sour milk your cake will be more tender, but you must use only soda and no cream tartar; if you prefer to use yeast powder instead of soda and cream tartar, two teaspoons of yeast powder are equal to one of soda and two of cream tartar, and should be put in the flour. Yeast powder is always safer to give servants to use, as they are very apt to use too much soda, though yeast powder cake will dry much quicker than cake made of soda and cream tartar.

WHITE SPONGE, OR ANGELS' FOOD CAKE.

Whites of eleven eggs, one and one-half tumblers of granulated sugar, one tumbler of sifted flour, one teaspoonful of vanilla, one teaspoonful of cream tartar; sift the flour four times, add the cream tartar and sift again. Beat the eggs to a stiff froth on a large platter; on the same platter add the sugar lightly, the flour very gently, then the vanilla; don't stop beating until ready for the pan. Bake forty minutes in a moderate oven. Try with a straw, and if too soft let it remain a few moments longer. Do not open the oven until the cake has been in fifteen minutes; the cake pan should not be greased. Tumbler for measuring should hold two and a quarter gills. When cooked turn the pan upside down to cool; remove the cake by cutting around the sides of the pan with a knife. When the ingredients are measured make all possible haste to get it quickly into the oven with the least beating possible, just enough to properly mix the eggs, sugar, and flour—on this rests the secret of success.

SILVER CAKE.

One cup of butter, two cups of sugar, three and one-half cups of flour, one cup of sweet milk, the whites of five eggs well beaten, two teaspoonfuls of baking powder; flavor to taste. J. R. L.

SPREAD MOUNTAIN CAKE.

To the yolks of five eggs, well beaten, add one cup of sugar, one-half cup of butter, one-half cup sweet milk, one teaspoonful of cinnamon, one grated nutmeg, then the whites of two eggs well beaten, then one and one-half cups of flour in which has been sifted two teaspoonfuls of baking powder. Bake in jelly cake pans; when cold spread each layer with an icing made with the whites of three eggs and one and one-half teacups of powdered sugar.

RIBBON CAKE.

Two and a half cups of sugar, one cup of butter, one cup of sweet milk, four cups of flour, four eggs, one-half teaspoon of soda. Divide the cake when mixed. For the dark portion, add one cup of currants and raisins, one large spoonful of molasses, and spice to taste; flavor the light with vanilla; put in alternate layers of dark and light in the bake pans. MRS. PRINCE, Dublin, N. H.

MARTHA WASHINGTON TEA CAKE.

One and one-fourth pounds of white sugar, one and one-half pounds of butter, two pounds of flour, one pint of sour milk, six eggs, one teaspoonful of soda in the sour milk, grated rind of two lemons and juice of one lemon, one nutmeg, a little mace, one pound of raisins, one pound of currants, one and a half pounds of citron. Whip the butter and sugar to a cream, to which add the yolks of the eggs well beaten; then put in the milk and flour alternately; then the whites of the eggs beaten to a froth; have the fruit floured and stir in last. Bake two and one-fourth hours; cover with a buttered paper to keep from browning too fast. This recipe is said to have been used by Mrs. Martha Washington.

Mrs. Stephen Gardner.

PORTSMOUTH BLACK CAKE.

Two pounds of flour, two pounds of sugar, two pounds of butter, two pounds of raisins, three pounds of currants, one pound of citron, twenty-one eggs, four nutmegs, two teaspoonfuls of cinnamon, two teaspoonfuls of allspice, two teaspoonfuls of mace, one large wine-glassful of brandy, one and a half wine-glassfuls of wine and rose-water mixed, one lemon. Brown the flour slightly, use brown sugar, bake five hours.

Mrs. Wentworth.

FRUIT CAKE.

Four pounds of seeded raisins, two pounds of currants, two cups of butter, one cup of citron, two cups of milk or half a cup of brandy, four cups of brown sugar, twelve eggs, six teaspoonfuls of yeast powder, two quarts of flour; spice to taste.

Mrs. S. C. Cummins.

BLACK CAKE.

Two pounds of dredged currants, two pounds of stoned raisins, one pound of flour, one tablespoonful of cinnamon, one tablespoonful of mace, four nutmegs, two glasses of wine, one glass of brandy, one glass of rose-water, one pound of citron, one pound of loaf sugar, one pound of butter, twelve eggs. Beat the butter and sugar to a cream, stir the eggs in gradually, add the flour and fruits, spices and liquors by degrees, bake in a moderate oven at least four hours; if in large cakes, leave in the oven to cool. Ice it the next morning; first dredge the cake with flour, then wipe with a towel; this will make the icing stick.

Mrs. Mary Copp and Mrs. G. F. Filley.

SPONGE CAKE.

Take any number of eggs, their weight in sugar (powdered is best), and half their weight in flour, the rind and juice of three lemons to an even pound of eggs.

Mrs. F. G. Goddard.

SPONGE CAKE.

One dozen of eggs, one pound of sugar, three-quarters of a pound of flour (light weight), the rind of two and juice of one good sized lemon; break the eggs, whites and yolks together, in a large bowl, add the sugar, and juice and rind of the lemons; beat the mixture briskly for half an hour with an egg-beater, then stir in very lightly the flour, and bake in a moderate oven—one suitable for bread.

Miss Krum.

SPONGE CAKE.

Seven eggs, whites and yolks together, three-quarters of a pound of sugar dissolved in half a tumbler of water, let it melt, and just come to a boil; half a pound of flour, one teaspoonful of yeast powder, one teaspoonful of extract of lemon; beat eggs and sugar together until very light, then add the flour.

Miss Albright, Kirkwood, and Mrs. Smithers.

BREAD CAKE.

One pint of sponge, two teacups of sugar, one teacup of butter, three eggs, one teaspoonful of soda; fruit, spice to taste; flour depends upon the thickness of the sponge.

Mrs. Grace Helm.

SPONGE CAKE.

Six eggs beaten together very light; add slowly three tea-cups of sugar and three of flour; in the last cup of flour put one teaspoonful of yeast powder; the very last thing add one cup of boiling water; flavor with lemon; bake one hour. Mrs. R. H. Morton.

CONNECTICUT LOAF CAKE.

Six pounds of flour, three pounds of sugar, three pounds of butter, one and a half ounces of mace, five eggs, three pounds of raisins, stoned, four nutmegs, one pint home-made yeast, two lemons, one wine-glass of brandy; beat half the quantity of butter and sugar to a cream, add the flour wet with half the quantity of yeast; mix it quite soft, and let it stand till risen very light; add the rest of the ingredients, and let it rise again, then stir in lightly the raisins, dredged with flour, and bake. The above will make eight loaves. Mrs. G. F. Filley.

WHITE FRUIT CAKE.

Three cups of sugar, one large cup of butter, the whites of twelve eggs, five cups of sifted flour, one full cup of sweet milk, two pounds of raisins boiled till the water is all boiled away; flour the raisins well with extra flour; one large spoonful of yeast powder, one wine-glass of brandy.
Mrs. Kennaday, New York.

CHOCOLATE CAKE.

Two cups of sugar, one cup of butter, one cup of sweet milk, three and a half cups of flour, two teaspoonfuls of baking powder, five eggs, whites of two left out for frosting; bake in a large dripping pan.

Frosting.—Beat the whites of the two eggs, add one cup of sugar, four tablespoonfuls of chocolate, two teaspoonfuls of vanilla; put on while hot.

CAKES.

CHOCOLATE CAKE.

Use velvet cake baked in layers; for filling use one-half cake of Baker's chocolate, one cup of sugar, one-half pint of sweet milk, a small piece of butter; boil until stiff enough; when cool, flavor with vanilla.

WHITE CAKE.

The whites of sixteen eggs, three cups of sugar, one cup of milk, four cups of flour, one level teaspoonful of soda, two heaping teaspoonfuls of cream tartar, not quite a half cup of butter, rose-water; sift flour and sugar before measuring, rub cream tartar thoroughly through flour, dissolve soda in milk, bake in a slow oven. This rule makes a very large cake.   Mrs. S. C. Cummins.

VELVET CAKE.

One pound of sugar, one pound of flour, half a pound of butter, four eggs, one teacup of cold water, one teaspoonful of cream tartar, half a teaspoonful of soda, flavor with extract of lemon; beat the sugar and butter to a white cream, dissolve the soda in the water, and sift the cream tartar into the flour, mixing thoroughly; add to the butter and sugar the pound of flour and the water, beat it all well; beat the eggs, the yolks first and then the whites, to a stiff froth; beat them together for a minute, and stir into the cake; beat the cake well for about three minutes; bake an hour. This will make two loaves. It may be flavored with nutmeg and spices, or with raisins and currants, or be made into delicious chocolate cake by being baked in layers and filled with chocolate frosting. It makes nice jelly cake.
    Mrs. Sam'l Copp.

ALMOND CAKE.

One dozen eggs, one-half pound of almonds, one-half grated fine, one-half cut fine, one pound of powdered sugar, one-fourth pound of citron cut fine, a dessert spoonful of cloves, cinnamon and allspice each, one saucer full of stale rye bread crumbs. To mix the cake, beat eight whites to a stiff froth, and after beating the rest of whites and yolks together stir into them the other ingredients, adding the whites last; bake three-fourths of an hour. This cake should be stirred one way only.

APPLE CAKE.

Soak in water over night three cups of dried apples; pour off the water and chop fine; boil them in three cups of molasses one-half hour; when taken from the stove add one teaspoonful of soda; stir well; when cool add one cup of butter, three cups of flour, one cup of sugar, three eggs, one tablespoonful of cinnamon and cloves, nutmeg and any spice you wish, and flavoring with wine or brandy, and fruit, as much or little as you like; or make it without fruit, other than the apples, which makes it quite moist and rich-looking like citron. Bake from one to two hours in a slow oven.

Mrs. H. Waterman.

SPICED MARBLE CAKE.

The whites of seven eggs, three cups of white sugar, one cup of butter, four cups of flour, one cup of sour cream, a small teaspoonful of soda.

The yolks of seven eggs, two cups of brown sugar, one cup of molasses with a small teaspoonful of soda in it, one cup of butter, five cups of flour, one cup of sour cream, one teaspoonful of soda; cloves, allspice, cinnamon to taste. Half this quantity of dark is sufficient for the white top and bottom.

Mrs. R. H. Morton.

MARBLED CAKE—Two Cards.

LIGHT PART.

One and a half cups of light sugar, half a cup of butter, half a cup of sweet milk, half a teaspoonful of soda, one teaspoonful of cream of tartar, whites of four eggs, two and a half cups of flour; beat the eggs with the sugar, add the butter melted, put the soda, cream and milk together, then add the flour.

CAKES.

DARK PART.

One cup of brown sugar, half a cup of molasses, half a cup of butter, half a cup of sour milk, half a teaspoonful of soda, one teaspoonful of cream of tartar, yolks of four eggs, two and a half cups of flour, one teaspoonful of cloves, one of cinnamon, one of nutmeg, one of allspice; beat and mix same as the light part. When each part is ready, drop a spoonful of dark, then of light, upon the bottom of the pan in which it is to be baked, and so proceed till the pan is full.

Mrs. G. F. Filley.

MARBLE CAKE.

Eight eggs, three cups of the best white sugar, two cups of butter, six cups of flour; put the whites of the eggs in one pan, the yolks in another, with half of the butter, sugar and flour; beat till very light; then divide the white part, take a teaspoonful of cochineal, pour a little boiling water to it; when it is a bright rose color, color half of the white with it; flavor the yellow with lemon, the white with almond, the pink with rose-water; put it in the pan in layers; frost as soon as taken from the oven.

Mrs. Haskell.

CHOCOLATE MARBLE CAKE.

One cup of butter, two cups of sugar, three cups of flour, five eggs, half a cup of milk, one teaspoonful of yeast powder; take out one cup of the dough, and mix grated chocolate wet with a little milk; flavor the chocolate with vanilla, and drop in spots as marble cake; flavor the light part of the cake with nutmeg.

Mrs. R. H. Morton.

SILVER CAKE.

Two cups of fine white sugar, two and a half cups of sifted flour, half a cup of butter, three-quarters of a cup of sweet milk, the whites of eight eggs, half a teaspoonful of soda, a teaspoonful of cream tartar; flavor with either almond or lemon.

Mrs. E. F. Richards.

GOLD CAKE.

Cream one cup of sugar and three-quarters of a cup of butter together very light, add half a cup of milk, the yolks of eight eggs beat very light, two cups of sifted flour, half a teaspoonful of soda, one teaspoonful of cream tartar; flavor with lemon. MRS. PETTES AND OTHERS.

DOVER CAKE.

Six eggs, one pound of sugar, one-half pound of butter, one pound of flour, one cup of milk, two teaspoonfuls of yeast powder. MRS. H. B. L.

DELICATE CAKE.

Two cups of white sugar, three-quarters of a cup of butter, three-quarters of a cup of milk, whites of eight eggs, three cups of flour, three teaspoonfuls of baking powder; flavor to taste. MRS. C.

PLAIN FRUIT CAKE.

Two and a half cups of sugar, three-quarters of a cup of butter, one cup of milk, five eggs beaten separately, five cups of flour, two teaspoonfuls of baking powder, two and a half pounds of raisins, allspice, cloves, nutmeg and cinnamon to taste; bake in a quick oven. MISS A. F.

CHOCOLATE CREAM CAKE.

To the yolks of four eggs, well beaten, add two cups of white sugar, one cup of butter, one cup of sweet milk, three cups of flour having in it one measure of "Banner" baking powder; then add the whites of four eggs well beaten; bake in jelly cake pans.

FOR THE CREAM.—To four ounces of plain chocolate, grated, add one cup of white sugar, two tablespoonfuls of corn starch, one cup of sweet milk, one tablespoonful of extract of vanilla; mix well together and boil until it thickens, stirring constantly; when cold, spread it on the layers of the cake.

LADY CAKE.

One pound of sugar, three-quarters of a pound of butter, one pound of flour, whites of sixteen eggs beaten light; cream the butter and sugar together, then mix the eggs three or four at a time, then the flour.

MOLASSES PLUM CAKE.

One cup of butter, one cup of sugar, one cup of molasses, one cup of milk, two eggs, four cups of flour, one teaspoonful of soda stirred in the molasses, one teaspoonful of cloves, cinnamon and nutmeg. MRS. T. T. RICHARDS.

HICKORY NUT CAKE.

One and a half cups of sugar, half a cup of butter, two cups of flour, three-fourths of a cup of sweet milk, one cup of hickory nuts, one teaspoon cream of tartar, one-half teaspoon of soda, whites of four eggs.
MRS. S. C. DAVIS.

RAILROAD CAKE.

One cup of sugar, one cup of flour, three eggs, three tablespoonfuls of butter, three tablespoonfuls of milk, one teaspoonful of baking powder. MRS. H. D. HATCH.

LUNCH CAKE.

One cup of sugar, butter the size of an egg, one cup of milk, one egg, three cups of flour, one-third of a cup of cocoanut, raisins or currants. MRS. W. H. PULSIFER.

BRIDE'S CAKE.

Two cups of sugar, one-half cup of butter, the whites of five eggs beaten to a stiff froth, one cup of cold water; mix well together; then add three cups of flour into which one teaspoon of soda and two of cream tartar have been stirred; beat briskly for two minutes; flavor with almond, and bake in a quick oven; frost the top. S. NOYES.

CORN STARCH CAKE.

One cup of butter, two of sugar, one of sweet milk, two cups of flour, one cup of corn starch, whites of seven eggs, half a teaspoonful of soda, one of cream tartar; beat the butter and sugar to a cream.
Mrs. H. C. Moore and others.

WATER POUND CAKE.

One cup of butter, three cups of sugar, four cups of flour, six eggs, one cup of water or milk, one teaspoonful of yeast powder.
Mrs. Morton.

EGGLESS CAKE.

Two cups of sugar, two cups of buttermilk, two cups of raisins, one-half cup of butter, one tablespoonful of soda, four cups of flour; spice as you like.
Mrs. Treat.

TEN EGG CAKE.

The whites of ten eggs, two cups of sugar, one cup of butter, four cups of flour, one cup of milk, one teaspoonful of soda and two of cream of tartar; flavor with almond.
Mrs. O. D. Filley.

CREAM CAKE.

Four cups of flour, three cups of sugar, one cup of cream, five eggs, one teaspoonful of saleratus, one cup of butter; mix the sugar and butter together, add the rest.

QUEEN CAKE.

One pound of flour, three-quarters of a pound of sugar, one-half pound of butter, one pound of fruits, one wine-glass of brandy, one wine-glass of wine, one wine-glass of milk, four eggs, one-half teaspoonful of soda.
Mrs. Joseph Shippen and Mrs. S. Copp.

FANNY CAKE.

One and a half cups of sugar, half a cup of butter, half a cup of milk, three eggs, two cups of flour, one teaspoonful of yeast powder.
Mrs. W. H. Pulsifer.

CUP CAKE.

One cup of butter, two cups of sugar, four cups of flour, one cup of milk, six eggs, whites beaten separately, one teaspoonful of soda and two of cream of tartar; flavor as you like. Is very nice with fruit.   Mrs. O. D. Filley.

CIDER SPICE CAKE.

One heaping cup of sugar, one-half cup of butter, one egg, one cup of cider with one teaspoonful of soda stirred in, two teaspoonfuls of cinnamon, one teaspoonful of cloves, one-half cup of raisins, chopped; extract of lemon.
    Mrs. E. Brown, Connecticut.

WHITE CAKE.

The whites of thirty-six eggs, nine cups of sugar, three cups of milk, three cups of butter, five cups of flour, six teaspoonfuls of yeast powder; flavor with almond. This makes a very large loaf suitable for company.
    Mrs. S. C. Cummins.

SPICE CAKE.

One and a half cups of butter, three cups of sugar, one cup of milk, five cups of flour, five eggs, one teaspoonful of powdered cinnamon, one teaspoonful of cloves, allspice and nutmeg, one teaspoonful of soda, one pound of stoned raisins; beat the eggs, sugar and milk together, then add the other articles.   Mrs. Kline.

MUNSON CAKE. "VERY NICE."

Two cups of sugar, half a cup of butter, four eggs, one cup of milk, four small cups of flour, half a nutmeg grated, two cups of raisins, one teaspoonful of yeast powder; stir the butter and sugar to a cream, mix the yeast powder thoroughly with the flour, add alternately the flour, eggs and milk, a little at a time; beat the mixture well, and having dredged the raisins with flour, put them in just before turning into the pans; bake in a moderate oven for three-quarters of an hour.   Miss Maggie Krum.

SHREWSBURY CAKE.

Rub to a cream half a pound of butter and three-quarters of a pound of sugar and five well beaten eggs, a nutmeg or a teaspoonful of rose-water, and a quart of flour. When well mixed drop with a spoon on buttered tins and sift on powdered sugar, then put on small pieces of citron and raisins. MRS. T. J. ALBRIGHT.

WARREN CAKE.

One pint of sugar, one cup of butter, three eggs, one quart of flour, two teaspoonfuls of cream tartar in part of the flour, one teaspoonful of soda in a cup of milk, one pound of raisins, a little brandy, nutmeg, cloves, cinnamon, etc.; if not thin enough, add a little more milk. A little molasses makes it dark colored. Bake it slow.
MRS. T. T. RICHARDS.

COFFEE CAKE, "VERY NICE."

Two teacups of sugar, one teacup of molasses, one teacup of butter, one teacup of cold coffee, five cups of flour, four eggs, two teaspoonfuls of cloves, mace, cinnamon, half a pound of chopped raisins, two teaspoonfuls of soda.
MRS. WELLS.

LINCOLN CAKE.

Two cups of sugar, half a cup of butter, one cup of milk, two eggs, three cups of flour, one teaspoonful of extract of lemon, one teaspoonful cream tartar, half a teaspoonful of soda. MRS. L. E. KLINE.

COCOANUT CAKE.

One pound of fine sugar, half a pound of butter, three-quarters of a pound of flour, six eggs, one large or two small cocoanuts, grated without the milk; cream the butter and sugar together, add the yolks of the eggs, then the whites, then the flour; mix well, and just before baking add cocoanut; bake in two long tins. MISS JULIA ROBERTS.

CAKES.

ALMOND CAKE.

Two pounds of sugar, one pound of butter, twelve eggs, one pound of flour, one pound of almonds blanched and pounded fine, two tablespoonfuls of rose-water; bake in thin sheets. MRS. WENTWORTH.

SODA CAKE.

Two and a half cups of sugar, three and a half cups of flour, one cup of sweet milk, three eggs, one heaping tablespoonful of butter, two teaspoonfuls of yeast powder, one teaspoonful of extract of lemon. MISS E. L. GLOVER.

HARRISON CAKE.

Two cups of sugar, two cups of butter, one cup of milk, five cups of flour, half a cup of molasses, three eggs, one teaspoonful of saleratus, one pound of raisins, cloves, cinnamon, nutmeg; a wine-glass of brandy improves it.
MRS. MCKITTRICK.

DATE CAKE.

Two tumblers of brown sugar, one and a half tumblers of butter, one tumbler of molasses, four tumblers of flour, six eggs, one pound of currants, half a pound of citron, one pound of dates, half a wine-glass of water, half a teaspoonful of soda, spice and lemon; bake three hours.

FEATHER CAKE.

Two cups of sugar, three eggs, butter size of an egg, one cup of milk, one spoonful of cream tartar, half a teaspoonful of soda, both put in with the milk, three cups of flour, one lemon; beat all twenty minutes. NOYES.

LEMON CAKE.

One cup of butter and three cups of sugar, beat to a froth yolks of five eggs, whites beaten separately, juice and rind of one lemon grated, four cups of flour, one cup of milk, one teaspoonful of soda.

NEW YORK GINGER BREAD.

One cup of milk, one cup of butter, two cups of sugar, three cups of flour, four eggs, six tablespoonfuls of ginger, one teaspoon of cream tartar, and one of soda.

Mrs. W. H. Pulsifer.

CARRIE'S GINGER BREAD.

One coffee-cup of molasses, one of sour milk or cream, one egg, one teaspoon of soda (heaped), one tablespoon of butter, one tablespoon of ginger, a little salt, not very stiff with flour; it will make two long tins.

Mrs. Wm. Maurice.

GINGER BREAD.

Two large teacupfuls of molasses, two small or one large cup of butter, one cup of sour milk, five cups of flour, two tablespoonfuls of ginger, and whatever other spices you wish, five eggs, half a teaspoonful of soda dissolved in the milk; stir the butter, sugar and spice in the molasses, then add the eggs, then the flour and milk; when done cut in large slices; pass around with lemonade.

Miss E. L. Glover.

SOFT GINGER CAKE.

Two pints of flour rounded, one pint of molasses; one-half pint of warm water, two tablespoonfuls of butter melted in the water, one large teaspoonful of soda, a little salt; flavor with cinnamon.

SOFT GINGER CAKE.

One-half cup each of sugar, molasses and butter, one cup of sour milk, two cups of flour, one egg, one teaspoon of ginger, one of soda. Miss Julia Roberts.

CRISP GINGER BREAD.

Three pounds of flour, one pound of sugar, three-quarters of a pound of butter, one pint of molasses, three tablespoonfuls of ginger; to be rolled out thin.

Miss E. L. Glover.

GINGER CRISPS.

One teacup of sugar, one teacup of molasses, one teacup of butter, one tablespoon of ginger, one teaspoon of soda dissolved in one-half teacup of vinegar, one egg, seven teacups of flour; bake in thin cakes for fifteen or twenty minutes.

GINGER SNAPS.

One cup of molasses and half a cup of butter brought to a boil, remove from fire and add one teaspoonful of salt, one teaspoonful of soda, and two teaspoonfuls of ginger; mix stiff; roll thin; bake quick and keep by themselves in a covered tin pail to remain crisp. J. R. A.

LAYER CAKES.

DAME DURDEN CAKE.

Half a cup of butter and two cups of sugar mixed to a cream, two eggs, one cup of milk with half a teaspoonful of soda, three cups of flour, one teaspoonful cream tartar; season with almond or lemon. This makes very nice cream or Washington pies, or two loaves of cake; split one twice and spread with chocolate icing.

ICING.—One-quarter of a cake of chocolate, half a cup of milk, one tablespoonful of corn starch; mix together, and cook over the teakettle until stiff, then sweeten to taste with powdered sugar, flavor with vanilla, and spread quickly.

JELLY ROLL.

One cup of flour, three-quarters of a cup of sugar, three eggs, one teaspoonful of butter, one teaspoonful of yeast powder.

LEMON JELLY FOR ROLL.—One cup of sugar, one egg, juice of one lemon, one tablespoonful of cold water; let it thicken on the stove, and stir while cooking.

MRS. L. E. KLINE.

MORENTIN CAKE.

Six eggs, two cups of sugar, four cups of flour, one cup of butter, one cup of milk, two teaspoonfuls of yeast powder; flavor with lemon; bake in four layers, the top ones each smaller, to form a pyramid; take the whites of three eggs to form the icing, putting some between, the balance over the top and sides; set in a cool oven to dry.

MRS. DERGANS.

ORANGE CAKE.

Two cups of sugar, two and a half cups of flour, one-half cup of cold water, three teaspoonfuls of baking powder, the yolks of five eggs, the whites of three, the rind and juice of one orange; bake in jelly cake tins.

ICING AND FILLING FOR SAME.—The whites of two eggs beaten light, the juice of one-half an orange and the rind of a whole one; make stiff with powdered sugar; put this between the layers and on top. MRS. R. H. MORTON.

LEMON CAKE.

One and a half cups of sugar, two cups of flour, three eggs beaten together, two teaspoonfuls of baking powder mixed with flour; add the last thing, half a cup of ice water; bake in jelly pans.

FILLING.—Three lemons, half a pound of sugar, two ounces of butter, three eggs: beat all together, put on the fire and stir till it thickens. MRS. S. C. DAVIS, JR.

GATEAU CITRON.

One pound of sugar, quarter of a pound of butter, six eggs, grated rind of two lemons, juice of three, boil till it thickens; when cold put it between two or three layers of sponge cake an inch thick, with a meringue on top.
MRS. D. YOUNG.

POVERTY CAKE.

One cup of sugar, a piece of butter size of an egg, half a cup of milk, two cups of flour, two eggs, one teaspoonful of soda, two teaspoonfuls of cream tartar, a little salt; bake in four jelly pans, and while warm spread with currant or plum jelly; makes a nice loaf, or it can be baked in two pans and used for cream or chocolate cakes. Cream: One cup of sugar, one pint of milk, two eggs, half a cup of flour; or it is nicer to use corn starch; boil the milk and stir in the eggs, sugar and flour mixed together. Chocolate: Instead of using all corn starch, use more than half grated chocolate; season with vanilla, spread on top as well as between the layers. This quantity of batter can be made into a loaf cake. MRS. J. C. PALMER AND RICHARDS.

CREAM FOR CAKE FILLING.

Half a pint of cream, half a cup of sugar, one teaspoonful of butter, sufficient corn starch to thicken it; put in a saucepan, set it in a pan of water, and cook it several minutes, stirring it hard all the while, then cool it and put in a teaspoonful of vanilla extract; spread it on your cake just as for jelly cake. E. M.

WASHINGTON PIE.

Four eggs beat separate, one teacupful of white sugar, butter the size of a walnut, three-quarters of a cup of milk or cream, one teaspoonful of soda, two teaspoonfuls of cream of tartar, three teacupfuls of flour; bake in jelly pans. Filling for same: One apple grated, one lemon grated, one egg, one teacupful of sugar; stir together over the fire five minutes, taking care not to burn; spread as jelly between layers of cake. MRS. POWELL.

THE QUEEN OF CREAM PIES.

Two teacups of flour, two of powdered sugar, nine eggs, one-half teaspoon of soda, one of cream tartar; mix the sifted flour, cream tartar and soda thoroughly dry; into the beaten yolks put one-half the sugar, and into the beaten whites the other half; then beat both together thoroughly; mix gradually with the flour; add lemon flavoring; pour into eight jelly pans. It will rise very light while in the oven, but don't be frightened if it falls after coming out, as it does not hurt it in the least.
MRS. W. FALLON.

CREAM.

Five eggs, one and a half teacups of powdered sugar, one cup not quite full of sifted flour, one quart rich milk; put the milk on to boil; beat the eggs all together; add the sugar, then the flour gradually; when well mixed pour over the milk, stirring constantly; put the dish in a pan of hot water on the stove and stir constantly until it is so thick that it will just pour out easily; will be thicker when cold; flavor with vanilla. MRS. W. FALLON.

ROLL CAKE.

One cup of flour, one cup of sugar, one teaspoonful of baking powder, four eggs; beat yolks of eggs and sugar together, add flour, then whites of eggs beaten very light; bake in a pan as large as the batter can be spread upon; bake in a quick oven; turn out: spread with jelly; roll while hot. Have a nice clean white cloth ready sprinkled with powdered sugar; roll it around the cake; let it remain until it gets cool. Bake twenty minutes.
MRS. D. R. POWELL.

WHITE MOUNTAIN CAKE.

One pound of flour, one pound of sugar, one-half pound of butter, one cup of sweet milk, the whites of ten eggs, two even teaspoonfuls of yeast powder; bake like jelly cake. Put icing and grated cocoanut between the layers, same over the top and sides. MRS. H. C. MOORE.

MOUNTAIN CAKE.

Cut any white or delicate cake you would use for jelly cake in as many layers as you wish, put between a thin frosting, on that strew a thick layer of cocoanut grated, then raisins chopped fine, then a thin layer of blanched almonds split open, then a layer of cake; continued till finished; frost the top, strewing the nut over the loaf.
MRS. H. WATERMAN.

CHOCOLATE CAKE.

One cup of sugar, half a cup of butter, one cup of milk, two cups of flour, whites of four eggs, three teaspoonfuls of yeast powder; bake as jelly cake. Filling: One cup of grated chocolate with two spoonfuls of pulverized sugar, whites of three eggs beaten to a stiff froth with two tablespoonfuls of sugar; mix with the chocolate and spread between the cakes when warm, over the top and sides, drying by stove. Miss LEE, Buffalo.

CREAM CAKES.

Two cups of cold water, one cup of butter, boil up once; then add two cups of flour while boiling, and stir until smooth; when cool, stir in six well beaten eggs and a little salt. Drop on buttered pan from a spoon. This will make about twenty cakes.

FILLING FOR CAKES.—Two cups of sugar, three-fourths cup flour, two eggs, two cups of milk. Beat the eggs, sugar and flour together, boil the milk and stir in the thickening, being careful not to let it burn. It is better to set the vessel into a kettle of boiling water and let it thicken gradually, flavor to suit the taste, vanilla or lemon, and fill the cakes when cold. L. F.

BOSTON CREAM CAKES.

The crust: One pint of boiling water, one cup of butter, four cups of flour, ten eggs; boil the water and butter together, stir in the flour while the water is boiling; when cool add the eggs well beaten, drop a spoonful at a time on your pan, then bake them; when done and cool, open them and put in the custard. The custard: One quart of milk, one cup of flour, two cups of sugar, four eggs; boil the milk, and while boiling add the sugar, then the flour and eggs well beaten together.

LEMON OR CHOCOLATE CAKE.

Three cups of sugar, one cup of melted butter, five eggs, one cup of milk, five cups of flour, three teaspoonfuls of yeast powder, lemon extract.

LEMON ICING.—Whites of two eggs, one cup of sugar, juice of two lemons and a little more than the grated rind of one lemon. This quantity makes two cakes of four layers.

Chocolate Custard for the same Cake.—One egg, one cup of sugar, one cup of milk, one cup of grated chocolate; stir all together and let it come to a good boil; when taken off add one and a half teaspoonfuls of vanilla; beat all very hard until quite smooth; when your cake is cold, spread on the chocolate.

Mrs. E. J. Clark, Carondelet.

MRS. GARDINER'S WHITE CAKE.

Three-quarters of a cup of butter, one cup of milk, two cups of sugar, three cups of flour, three-quarters of a cup of corn starch; whites of six eggs; mix with corn starch two teaspoonfuls of Price's baking powder; flavor with extract of almond; bake in thin cakes; make a thin icing and mix with grated cocoanut and spread between the layers. Use lemon extract if you make the cake with cocoanut.

DOUGHNUTS.

Stir into one pint of warm milk half a teacup of butter, the same of lard, flour enough to make a stiff batter, a teaspoonful of salt, and one cup of yeast; keep warm, and let it rise. When light work in two and a half cups of sugar, four eggs well beaten, two teaspoonfuls of cinnamon or nutmeg; knead well, adding flour until not quite as stiff as bread; let it rise again very light, roll out, cut in any shape desired, and fry in hot lard. Dredge with powdered sugar while hot. Mrs. O. D. Filley.

RAISED DOUGHNUTS.

One pint of warm milk, two-thirds of a cup of melted butter, half a cup of yeast; make a batter and let it rise over night; stir in, in the morning, two cups of sugar, four eggs, one teaspoonful of soda, two teaspoonfuls of cinnamon, a little salt, flour enough to make a dough; when light, fry.

Mrs. Wm. Maurice.

DOUGHNUTS.

One pint of sour cream, one teaspoonful of soda, one cup of sugar, one nutmeg, two eggs, flour enough to roll.
Mrs. F. G. Goddard.

YANKEE DOUGHNUTS.

Three pints of flour, one and a half teacups of sugar, one-third of a teacup of butter, two eggs, four teaspoonfuls of cream tartar, two teaspoonfuls of soda, one teaspoonful of extract of lemon, a little salt and milk; mould just stiff enough to roll out.
Mrs. G. F. Filley.

CRULLERS.

Four eggs, four tablespoonfuls of melted butter and lard, eight tablespoonfuls of sugar, one tablespoonful of yeast powder and half a cup of milk, flour sufficient to roll.
Mrs. N. H. Stevens.

CRULLERS.

Two cups of sugar, one cup of butter, one and a half cups of milk, five eggs, two teaspoonfuls of yeast powder, nutmeg; make soft to roll.
Mrs. S. R. Filley.

CRULLERS.

Two pounds of flour, three-quarters of a pound of sugar, half a pound of butter, six eggs, one cup of sweet milk (if you put milk it will take a little more flour), two teaspoonfuls of baking powder.
Mrs. Brock.

CRULLERS.

One teaspoonful saleratus in four tablespoonfuls of milk, one-half pint of flour, four tablespoonfuls of melted butter, one teaspoonful of salt; beat four eggs with eight heaping tablespoonfuls of white sugar, one nutmeg; work them into the rest with flour enough to make them cut, and fry in boiling lard.

MRS. CLARK'S CRULLERS.

Six eggs, six heaping tablespoonfuls of sugar, six tablespoonfuls of butter slightly warm; flour not too stiff; fry in hot lard. MRS. L. B. CLARK.

JUMBLES.

Two cups of sugar, one cup of butter, two eggs, one small teaspoonful of soda, one teaspoonful of cassia, flour sufficient to roll them. It is better to roll a part of them at a time, they are so rich and soft. N.

COOKIES.

Three cups of sugar, two cups of milk, three-fourths of a cup of butter, one teaspoonful of soda, two of cream tartar; one tablespoonful of cinnamon; flour enough to roll out. MILLY.

COOKIES.

Two cups of butter, two and a half cups of sugar, half cup of milk, four eggs; flavor to taste; whip the ingredients well; make into a stiff dough; two teaspoonfuls of yeast powder; roll thin; cut in design to suit; bake in a quick oven. Will keep nicely for ten days if kept dry.

MRS. RAINWATER.

NICE COOKIES WITHOUT EGGS.

One cup of butter, two of sugar, one of sweet milk, six of flour; flavor with cinnamon or nutmeg, and add from three to four teaspoonfuls of yeast powder; roll thin and bake. S. S. D.

VANILLA WAFERS.

One cup of sugar, two-thirds of a cup of butter, four tablespoonfuls of milk, one tablespoonful of vanilla, one egg, one and a half teaspoonfuls of cream tartar, two-thirds of a teaspoonful of soda, flour to roll out; roll very thin.

MRS. J. W. GODDARD.

MRS. ROBINSON'S COOKIES.

One-fourth pound of butter, one teaspoon of soda, caraway seed or nutmeg, one pound of sugar boiled in one-half pint of water; let it cool before mixing with the other ingredients; flour enough to stiffen to roll out thin.

LEMON COOKIES.

One pint of sugar, one cup of butter, three cups of flour, three eggs, one teaspoon of soda sifted into the flour, grated peel and juice of one lemon.

SCOTCH CAKES.

One pound of sugar, three-quarters of a pound of butter, three eggs, one nutmeg grated. To mix: Take about a pound of flour, with it mix the sugar and nutmeg, into this rub the butter, then add the eggs well beaten, and as much more flour as is necessary to roll them out very thin; the less flour used the more delicate the cakes will be.

MRS. F. G. GODDARD.

COCOANUT GEMS. "VERY NICE."

One cup of butter, three and a half cups of flour, two cups of sugar, four eggs, half a cup of milk, one cup of cocoanut. Use desiccated cocoanut, and soak it in the milk an hour or two before making the cakes. Bake in gem-pans, and do not fill the pans too full. MISS H.

MACAROONS.

Take one pound of blanched almonds pounded fine in a mortar, whip to a stiff froth the whites of four eggs, add two and a half pounds of sifted loaf sugar; mix these all well together; whip the whites of ten eggs more and add to the other; stir all together till very light, then drop them with a spoon on stiff white paper and lay on baking-tins in a slow oven; before putting in the oven, lay four or five pieces of sliced almonds on each macaroon.

MRS. FRANK FILLEY.

WAFERS.

Two cups of sugar, one cup of butter, half a cup of milk, half a teaspoonful of saleratus, flour to roll stiff and thin.
MRS. MAURICE.

SUGAR CAKES.

One-half pint of butter, one and one-half pints of sugar, two eggs, peel and grated rind of one lemon, one-half teaspoonful of soda dissolved in two tablespoonfuls of milk, a pinch of salt, flour enough to enable the dough to be rolled.
MRS. LEWIS E. KLINE.

COCOANUT JUMBLES.

Three-quarters of a pound of sugar, three-quarters of a pound of butter, one pound of flour, three eggs, one cocoanut grated. MISS S. M. STETSON, Boston.

SUGAR GINGER SNAPS.

Two cups of butter, four cups of sugar, one cup of milk, one teaspoonful of cream tartar, one teaspoonful of soda, two teaspoonfuls of ginger, one egg, flour enough to roll out; roll very thin, and bake in a quick oven.
MRS. F. A. DURGIN.

MOLASSES COOKIES.

Two cups of molasses, one cup of butter, four teaspoonfuls of soda, one tablespoonful of vinegar; ginger to taste; enough flour to roll thin. MRS. WM. MAURICE.

MY GINGER SNAPS.
THE GENTLEMEN'S FAVORITE.

One pint of melted butter, one pint of melted lard, one pint of sugar, one quart of molasses, five level tablespoonfuls of ginger, four quarts of flour, four teaspoonfuls of soda or eight teaspoonfuls of baking powder dissolved in a little sweet milk; roll out thin and bake. S. S. D.

GINGER DROPS.

One cup of butter, two cups of molasses, two eggs, two-thirds of a cup of milk, yeast powder, six cups of flour; cinnamon and ginger; bake in tins or gem-pans.
Mrs. Edgerton.

MOLASSES DROP CAKE.

One cup of molasses, half a cup of butter, three cups of flour, two teaspoonfuls of ginger, one teaspoonful of soda; beat the ingredients well together, and drop with a spoon in a buttered tin; bake quick.
Mrs. Davis.

HUNTING NUTS.

Little over three pints of flour, three-quarters of a tea-cup of butter, one teacup of sugar, one nutmeg, one-third of a cup of ginger, one-quarter of a teaspoonful of soda; rub together thoroughly and with molasses make a paste, not too stiff; roll it out in long strips; bake in a quick oven.
Mrs. G. F. Filley.

CRISPYS.

Two cups of sugar, one cup of butter, two eggs, half a cup of ginger, half a cup of milk, not quite half a teaspoonful of soda, flour enough to roll out thin; cut in small cakes, and bake in a pretty quick oven.
Mrs. Brock.

ICING.

To one pound of powdered white sugar, put the beaten whites of four eggs; beat the whites very light and stir in the sugar by degrees; flavor with lemon and spread on the cake with a knife dipped into cold water.

BOILED ICING.

Boil one pound of sugar in half a pint of water until it will string from the spoon; then pour it over the whites of four eggs beaten to a stiff froth and beat until cold; flavor; apply with a wet knife.
Mrs. C. B. Richards.

ICING.

One tablespoon of gelatine, one tablespoon of hot water, three tablespoons of cold water, sixteen tablespoons of sugar.
Mrs. J. W. Goddard.

CHOCOLATE CAKE ICING.

One pound white sugar dissolved in a little water and boil until it can be pulled when tried in cold water, the whites of four eggs beaten to a stiff froth; pour the boiling sugar upon the whites and stir constantly until cool; grate one and a fourth blocks of a cake of Baker's chocolate and stir in; use cake baked in jelly tins and spread chocolate icing between each layer of cake and then over the whole. Very nice. Mrs. R. H. Morton.

CAKE WITH COCOANUT ICING.

Use cake baked in jelly tins; grate one good sized cocoanut; boil a pound of sugar in a little water until it can be pulled when tried in cold water; the whites of four eggs beaten to a stiff froth; pour the boiling sugar upon the whites and stir constantly until cool, then add the grated cocoanut, reserving enough of it to decorate or frost the outside of the loaf; spread the icing between each layer of cake and over the whole, covering the sides, then spread lightly the reserved cocoanut over the whole. Delicious.
Mrs. R. H. Morton.

ICE CREAM, ETC.

ICE CREAM.

Three eggs, one quart of milk; let the milk come to a boil; beat the eggs and add one cup of sugar and about a teaspoonful of arrowroot; then pour the mixture into the milk and let it stay till smooth, but not long enough to boil again. Flavor when cold. MRS. S. C. DAVIS.

ICE CREAM.

One quart of milk, one quart of cream; take out two or three tablespoonfuls of the milk and set the rest to boil; dissolve one and a half tablespoonfuls of arrowroot in the cold milk, and when the milk boils mix the arrowroot well with it; just before taking from the fire add one pound of sugar; set away to cool; just before freezing whip the cream and flavor; mix all together. Let the mixture stand a while in the freezer before turning to let it get thoroughly cold.
MRS. SARAH DAVIS.

FRENCH ICE CREAM.

One quart of milk, one quart of cream, one-quarter of a box of gelatine, one pound of sugar, one teaspoon of vanilla; dissolve the gelatine in milk; let it come to a simmer; add the sugar; let it cool; then add cream and vanilla, whipping it thoroughly. Freeze like other ice cream.
MRS. LEWIS E. KLINE.

ITALIAN CREAM.

One ounce of gelatine, one quart of milk, eight eggs, one pint of cream, quarter of a pound of sugar; flavor with vanilla, and freeze. MISS SEMPLE.

STRAWBERRY ICE CREAM.

Make a boiled custard of one quart of milk, one teaspoonful of corn starch, two eggs, one cup of sugar; press three pints of strawberries, or as many more as you please, through a sieve; make the juice very sweet, add it, with one quart of cream, one cup of sugar, the whites of two eggs well whipped, to the custard just as you put it into the freezer. This makes one gallon of cream.
MRS. COONS.

WALNUT ICE CREAM.

One quart of cream, half a pound of sugar, three eggs, two ounces of English walnut meats, whip eggs and sugar, pour in cream; warm over the fire till it commences to thicken, pound walnuts fine, mix with the above; freeze in moulds.
REVERE HOUSE, Boston.

BISCUIT GLACE.

To half a pound of powdered sugar, add the yolks of four eggs and vanilla flavoring; beat well and add to two quarts of well whipped cream; color some of it red and spread on the bottom of paper capsules and fill up with fresh cream; then put them in a tin box with cover and pack well up on all sides with pounded ice and salt; let stand for two hours. It is then ready for use.

FROZEN PUDDING.

Three pints of milk, nine eggs; make a custard; one-quarter of a pound each of currants, raisins, citron, brandy peaches, one teaspoonful of arrowroot, one-quarter of a pound of chocolate; sweeten to taste and freeze.

FROZEN PEACHES.

Get soft, ripe freestones, peel and mash them through a cullender, sweeten very sweet, as the freezing makes them lose some sweetness. Then to make ice cream, add equal quantities of cream, with sugar sufficient for both. This is delicious. All fruits can be done in the same way, with more or less sugar.
MISS S. LARKIN.

PRESERVES AND CANNED FRUITS.

In selecting fruit for preserving and canning, always see that it is fresh and firm. If you wish your preserves to look clear and bright, use the best loaf or granulated sugar; if for more common use, an inferior quality of sugar may be used, but it will not look so well and is more apt to spoil. The porcelain kettle is the best for preserving, and should be rather broad than deep, for fruit cannot be done equally if too much heaped. Always keep your preserves in a dry place; should you see, after they have been kept a while, a coat of mould on the surface, you need not throw them away until you have first tried to recover them by adding a little more sugar and boiling them over again; but if they have an unpleasant smell and insects about them, then they must be thrown away. Keep preserves in small glass jars, as frequent opening injures them.

Jellies are all made nearly in the same manner, using the juice of the fruit and allowing a pound of sugar to a pint of juice. Jelly-bags should be made of white flannel; the bag should be first dipped in hot water, for if dry it will absorb too much of the juice.

Canned fruit requires much less sugar than preserving, and is considered by many a great improvement upon the old-fashioned way of preserving, as it retains more of its natural flavor and is certainly more economical. In making the syrup for canned fruits, take a quarter of a pint of sugar to one pint of water; will make syrup enough for one quart can.

PRESERVED QUINCES.

Pare and core your quinces, taking out the knotty and defective parts, cut them in quarters, weigh your fruit, allowing three-quarters of a pound of sugar to a pound of fruit, put the pieces in your preserving-kettle, cover them with the parings and a very little water, lay a large plate over them, boil till they are tender; take out the quinces, strain the liquor through a bag; boil the juice and sugar together about ten minutes, skimming it well, put in the quinces, boil them gently until they are quite clear and soft, take them out and spread them on large flat dishes; afterwards put them in glass jars, boil the syrup a few minutes longer, pour the syrup warm over them. You may boil by themselves the cores and parings, in as much water as will cover them well, till they are entirely dissolved, then strain them through a linen bag; while hot stir in as much powdered loaf sugar as will form a thick jelly. To keep quinces well requires plenty of rich syrup.

PRESERVED CHERRIES.

Remove the pits, allow a pound of sugar to a pound of fruit; put a layer of fruit in a preserving-kettle, then a layer of sugar; continue thus until all are in; boil until clear; put them in bottles while hot and seal them.

GREEN GAGE PLUMS.

Take an equal quantity of fruit and sugar, pour boiling water on the plums and wipe them dry, prick them, then make a syrup of the sugar and one-half pint of water; when it boils put in half the plums, let them do slowly until they look clear, then take them out and put in the balance. If the syrup is thin, boil it longer.

PRESERVED PEARS.

Pare, core and quarter the pears, and put into the kettle, just cover them with water, and let them simmer until soft; take them out and put three-quarters of a pound of sugar to a pint of water, and let it boil; put in the pears, and let them simmer until the sugar has penetrated the pears, or about ten or fifteen minutes. MRS. M. J. DAVIS.

CITRON MELON PRESERVES.

Peel and slice the melon thin; to every pound allow a pound of sugar; to six pounds of melon allow one-quarter of a pound of ginger root; boil the melon with two teaspoonfuls of soda until soft; when cold soak in strong alum water one hour; boil the ginger root in a syrup of one pint of water to two pounds of sugar, and skim well, then put the melon in and cook until preserved.

Mrs. E. F. Richards.

STEWED CRANBERRIES.

For one quart, make a syrup of one pint of water to two cups of sugar; let it scald, and then drop in your cranberries.

Mrs. Mary Copp.

PRESERVED PEACHES.

Take a firm clingstone peach, cut it round; with the hands twist it round so that it will separate, as the stone will adhere to one side, cut it out with a knife, peel the pieces, then weigh your fruit; allow three-quarters of a pound of sugar to one pound of fruit; lay them on a platter, sprinkle part of the sugar over them, let them stand three or four hours, pour off the juice into the preserving kettle, add the remaining sugar; when scalding hot put in the peaches, and boil fifteen or twenty minutes, until they look clear. Put in glass jars. The flavor is improved by taking a few of the pits, blanch them and let them boil with the fruit.

GRAPE PRESERVES.

With your fingers press each pulp from the skin; boil the pulp about ten minutes, then strain through a cullender to separate the seeds from the pulp; put skins, pulp and sugar together, and boil until jellied, allowing three-quarters of a pound of sugar to one pound of fruit; weigh the fruit after the seeds are out. You will find the Concord grape will make the best preserves.

Mrs. Glover.

PRESERVED PLUMS.

Take the large red plum, allowing three-quarters of a pound of sugar to one pound of fruit; put them in a stone jar or crock, a layer of plums, then a layer of sugar, so on till the jar is full; place a plate on top, set in the oven with a slow fire, let them cook slowly all day; when done take them out, put in glass jars, seal up for winter use.   MISS E. M. TUCKER.

PRESERVED APPLES FOR TEA.

Make a nice syrup of sugar and water, and put in it a small piece of ginger root; have some nice apples peeled and halved, pippins are the best to use; when the syrup has scalded up three or four times, drop in the apples, and let them stay until transparent. Pie-plant is also very nice prepared in this way.

GOOD APPLE SAUCE.

Peel, quarter and core as many apples as you desire, put them in a vessel with water enough to keep them from burning, add half a cup of sugar; flavor them either with grated nutmeg, cinnamon, or grated rind of a lemon. After they are well cooked, just before pouring them into a dish, add a small lump of butter.

CRAB APPLE PRESERVE.

Make a syrup, allowing equal weight of sugar and apples; when the syrup becomes cool, put in the apples; boil them without crowding until they begin to grow soft; then take them up; boil the syrup in the course of three or four days and turn it on them while hot; repeat this after a few days until they appear to be thoroughly preserved.

BLACKBERRY JAM.

Three fourths of a pound of brown sugar to one pound of fruit; put on the stove and cook slowly most all day.

PRESERVED ORANGES.

Peel the oranges, boil them in water until you can run a straw through them; allow three-fourths of a pound of sugar for each pound of fruit; take the oranges from the water and pour the hot syrup over them; let them stand one night; the next day boil them in the syrup until it is thick and clear.   MRS. CLARA YOUNG.

TO PRESERVE STRAWBERRIES.

Hull the berries; to one pound of fruit, three-quarters of a pound of sugar; put the berries in the kettle; pour sugar over them; let them stand one hour; put them on the fire; let them boil twenty-five minutes as hard as they can boil; let them cool a little; put in jars. Cherries are done the same way, only one pound of sugar to one pound of fruit.
      MRS. BROCK.

PRESERVED CURRANTS.

Strip the currants off the stems; put a pint of sugar to a pound of currants; boil twenty minutes; then pour them in jars. Strawberries may be done in the same way, only putting a pint and a half of sugar to a pound of fruit.

COMBINATION JAM.

Two gallons of red cherries, one gallon of red raspberries, one gallon of currants; stone the cherries and cook down; add the raspberries and currants and cook again. To each quart add a pint of sugar and cook fifteen minutes.
      MRS. F. A. DURGIN.

CONSERVES.

Take any kind of fruit desired and pare it; then put one pound of fruit to one-half pound of white sugar; put in to stew and let it cook until the fruit begins to look right clear; then take a perforated spoon and take out the fruit (leaving the syrup on the fire and adding more fruit to it; if it does not taste sweet enough add a little more sugar) and drip it

until the juice is all out and spread it loosely on large flat dishes. Put the dishes in the oven after dinner, or when the oven is moderately warm, and let them remain a few hours, watching that the oven is not too hot. Repeat this for two or three days; when it seems very dry, so that it is brittle, sprinkle the finest powdered white sugar with a fine sifter over each piece and lay it in boxes for further use.
Mrs. Henderson, Md.

HODGE-PODGE.

Eight pounds of peaches, eight pounds of pears, eight pounds of quinces if in season, and two pounds of cantalope; pare six large lemons; boil the peel until tender; then cut peel and lemon into small pieces; to each pound of fruit put one-half pound of sugar; boil all well until quite smooth, or about two hours; either cling or freestone peaches will do. If the pairs and quinces are hard, they should be first boiled without sugar. Mrs. Geo. Henderson.

BAKED PEARS.

Take the hard preserving pear; boil until you can stick your fork through them easily; then put them into a baking pan, adding two tablespoonfuls of molasses, two of sugar, five or six whole cloves, a lump of butter; fill your pan nearly full of water; then bake them. Mrs. S.

PEACH MARMALADE.

Parboil the peaches and mash them fine; to every pint of peaches add one pint of white sugar and boil until clear.

PEACH BUTTER.

One peck of peaches, two quarts of boiled cider; reduce by boiling one gallon of sweet cider to one-half its quantity, pare and cut soft peaches, put into the preserving kettle with the cider, boil until they are reduced to a pulp, stirring constantly; if not sweet enough add a little sugar; cover tight in jars.

GRAPE BUTTER.

Prepare your fruit the same as for perserves, allowing a pound of sugar to a pound of fruit, a half pint of vinegar to three pounds of sugar; add a teaspoonful of cloves, nutmeg, cinnamon and allspice; boil until jellied, stirring it all the time. MRS. G.

PINEAPPLE BRANDY.

Prepare the pine-apple as for the table, cutting off the hard knots and slicing in thin pieces; allow one pound of white sugar to one pound of fruit; put it in glass jars, a layer of sugar, a layer of fruit; when your jar is full pour in white brandy until all the spaces are filled.

MRS. E. J. CLARK, Carondelet.

BRANDY PEACHES.

Three pints of water, with soda enough to make the water slippery, and let the water boil; scald the peaches about three minutes, enough to take the skins off, then rinse them in cold water and wipe with a coarse towel; make your syrup pound for pound; when done, put the peaches in and let them just scald, then turn off, and when half cooled put in brandy to suit and any kind of spices.

MRS. G. F. FILLEY.

GELATINE JELLY.

Soak one package of gelatine in a pint of cold water for twenty minutes, turn into a porcelain kettle, and add one quart of boiling water, one quart of white sugar; stir into this the beaten white of one egg; boil five minutes; season with one champagne glass of wine, or juice of two lemons; strain through a flannel bag into the mould.

MRS. G. F. FILLEY.

WINE JELLY.

One box of gelatine, two quarts of water (if the weather is cold, if not, three pints), three-quarters of a pound of white sugar, the juice and rind, but not the seeds, of six lemons, six eggs, the whites and yolks, six or eight sticks of cinnamon; put all these ingredients in a kettle and set it on the fire, and stir it hard till the gelatine is melted, then let it boil about fifteen minutes, add half a pint of good Madeira wine, strain it through a flannel bag until clear, and set it in your ice-chest or in a cool place.

COFFEE JELLY.

Three-quarters of a package of gelatine soaked in a little warm water, pour on one quart of hot strong coffee, two cups of sugar and a little lemon juice; strain, and set in moulds to cool. MISS S. L.

CHOCOLATE MANGE.

One quart of sweet milk, half a box of gelatine, half a cake of chocolate grated fine, one cup of sugar; mix and let dissolve; strain and set in a cool place; when quite cool add one cup of sweet cream, and put in a mould. MISS S. L.

STRAWBERRY, RASPBERRY AND BLACKBERRY JELLY.

The jelly of all these berries is made in a similar manner. Take the berries when ripe, mash them, and let them drain through a flannel bag; put a pint of juice to one pound of sugar and one-third the white of an egg, set it on the fire; on boiling up well, remove from the fire and skim it clear, if more scum arises take it off and skim again; boil until it becomes a jelly. On dropping a little into a tumbler of cold water, if it falls to the bottom in solid form it is jellied.

CIDER JELLY.

One box of gelatine, a scant quart of boiling water, two lemons, one quart of cider and one pint of sugar; put the gelatine and grated rind of the lemons together with the sugar, and pour over them the boiling water; let it dissolve, then add the cider and juice of the lemons; strain through a cloth into moulds and dishes.

MRS. A. M. GARDINER.

CRANBERRY, GRAPE AND CURRANT JELLY.

Pick your fruit from the stem, put them in a preserving kettle, let them boil until well broken up, then pour into a cullender; take the juice and strain through a flannel bag; allow a pint of sugar to a pound of fruit; before adding the sugar boil the juice ten minutes; while the juice is boiling, warm the sugar by putting it in a pan in the oven; then put the sugar to the juice, let boil ten or fifteen minutes; pour while hot into glass tumblers.

APPLE JELLY.

TWENTY GLASSES.

One peck and a half of good juicy apples (pippins), one dozen of lemons; cut the lemons, extract the seeds, and pare and core the apples, and then boil together till they are mush; strain, and allow one pound of sugar to one pint of juice, and boil twenty-five minutes.

Mrs. E. H. Semple.

TO CAN TOMATOES WHOLE.

Scald and pare the tomatoes, set them in pans in the oven until thoroughly heated; if very large take out the core, that they may heat more readily; when done lift carefully into the cans, and cover with the liquor that is found in the pans; if there is not enough of this, mash up another tomato to obtain more. Tomatoes put up in this manner can be sliced and eaten with vinegar as in summer.

Aunt Mary.

WINE JELLY.

Take a box of refined gelatine, and pour upon it a pint of cold water, after soaking ten minutes, add a pint of boiling water, stir it until the gelatine is dissolved; next add a pint of good wine and three-quarters of a pound of sugar, the juice of two lemons, and boil the rinds of the lemons with pieces of cinnamon in a small quantity of water, and

add the mixture; then beat the whites of two eggs and stir into it, put it on the fire and let it boil for a minute; when taken up let it stand for a few moments, then strain it through a jelly-strainer, with cloth well rinsed in boiling water, returning the mixture until it comes out perfectly clear.
MRS. HUGH CAMPBELL.

CANNING CORN AND TOMATOES.

You have heard of the nectar that's sipped by the gods;
I can tell you of something that's best by all odds,
And far more substantial, I know you'll allow,
So listen, and how to prepare it I'll show:

Take a peck of tomatoes fresh plucked from the vine,
The "Trophy," I think, you'll admit very fine,
Take the skins from their backs and their bodies thin slice,
Put into the pot, boil up twice or thrice;
Then condiments add, the salt and the pepper,
These serve the good purpose to keep them the better;
Have ready of corn three dozen large ears,
Of this being too much you need have no fears;
Let it be of its kind the sweetest and best,
If the seed's from Nantucket you safely may rest;
With sharp knife cut each grain right into the heart
('Tis well that this surgery causes no smart),
Then scrape the soft substance and milk from within,
And be careful to keep it quite free from the skin,
Next into the kettle and boil it awhile,
Fifteen minutes or twenty will do it in style;
Now into your cans you can put it in haste,
And leave at the top an inch of clear space;
This is said to be needed for holding the gas,
And without it there's danger of spoiling the "sass."

Next winter if Queen Vic. from over the sea,
Should honor herself by coming to "tea,"
Serve up some smoking hot, and she'll soon buy a book
And send it by telegraph straight to her cook.
A PRACTICAL HOUSEKEEPER.

CANNED GRAPES.

Take the Concord grape when fully ripe, stemming them without breaking any more than can be helped; allow a little over a quarter of a pound of sugar to a pound of fruit; make a syrup of about a quart of water at a time, putting in fruit enough for only one can; let your syrup, with the fruit in it, just come to a boil, putting them in the cans before they crack open: seal them up.

MISS E. L. GLOVER.

CANNED PEACHES.

The white Heath clings are preferred. Take white clings tolerably ripe, ring and pare them; pare only enough for four cans; make a syrup of half a pint of sugar to one quart of water (this quantity usually fills two one-quart cans). First put in your kettle the water, add the sugar, when that is dissolved put in the peaches, cook them a few minutes, or until a silver fork will enter them easily, but not enough for the fruit to break, then put in cans and seal immediately; can as soon as possible after peeling to prevent their discoloring by exposure to the air. Fruit of all kinds may be canned by the above rule excepting pears and quinces, which, if very hard, must first be boiled in clear water until tender, then make the syrup and let them boil a few minutes. The Bartlett pears, when nearly ripe, are very fine; they will not need boiling before putting into the syrup.

CANNED OCHRE AND TOMATOES.

To one peck of tomatoes take a quarter of a peck of ochre, slice the ochre, boil it first in a little water until tender, then add the tomatoes, boil both a few minutes, then put them in cans.

PICKLES.

In preparing pickles always use the best of cider vinegar. A porcelain kettle is the best to use; copper should be avoided, as it is poisonous; grape leaves are good to green them with, and a very little alum makes them brittle.

CUCUMBER PICKLES.

Put freshly picked cucumbers in cold, strong brine, sufficient to cover them; let them stand twenty-four hours; then turn off the brine; boil, skim and pour over the cucumbers again; repeat this every other day until the brine has been scalded three times; on the day following the last scalding throw away the brine and set the cucumbers, covered with fresh cold water, over the fire, first lining the kettle with grape leaves; cover the pickles closely with the leaves and put in the kettle a small piece of alum; scald (not boil) the pickles until they begin to turn green; then turn off the water; wipe the pickles; put them in jars and pour over them good cider vinegar that has been boiled fifteen minutes and well skimmed. Boil in the vinegar whole cloves, allspice, peppercorns and another small bit of alum. When cold, cork or seal the jars, and put in a cool place.
MRS. J. M. KRUM.

CUCUMBER PICKLES.

Make a brine not too strong, not strong enough to bear an egg, and pour over your cucumbers, hot; repeat this three times in nine days; take out of the brine; drain and wipe well; then put them in jars with your spices, horseradish, etc.; pour cold vinegar over them; let them stand three weeks before using
MRS. CORNELIA BEER.

PICKLED CUCUMBERS.

Wipe the cucumbers carefully; have ready stick cinnamon, cloves, allspice, mustard seed, celery seed, a little pulverized alum, small green peppers and salt; put in a stone jar a layer of pickles and a layer of spices, alternately, until the jar is filled; pour good cider vinegar over them until covered; tie brown paper tightly over the jar and put in a cool place; look at them from time to time to see that no scum rises. MRS. O. D. FILLEY.

TOMATO KETCHUP.

One peck of tomatoes, skin and stew in a tin or pewter vessel, with half a pint of vinegar, till quite soft; sift them, being careful to get all the pulps through; add four tablespoonfuls of salt, three tablespoonfuls of flour of mustard wet in a gill of vinegar, two tablespoonfuls of ground cloves, two tablespoonfuls of ground allspice, two and a half tablespoonfuls of black pepper, two teaspoonfuls of cayenne pepper; boil slowly one hour. MRS. W. H. PULSIFER.

TOMATO KETCHUP.

Half a bushel of tomatoes, peel off the skin and boil until done, strain them through a seive, then add half a tablespoonful of allspice, cloves and red pepper, half a pint of salt, half a pint of vinegar; cook down until thick.
MRS. JAMES BARTLETT.

MIXED PICKLES.

Equal portions of tomatoes, onions, cucumbers and cabbage sliced very thin, put in separate baskets and cover with salt, drip twelve hours, wash with cold water and mix white mustard seed, cloves and cinnamon; put in jars and cover with cold vinegar.

TOMATO KETCHUP.

Wipe the tomatoes and put them in a kettle, cover them close, and set them where they will become hot enough to burst; throw away the water; when the tomatoes are cool pass the pulp through a sieve. Measure the pulp, and to each quart add two-thirds of a wine-glass of salt, one-quarter of a wine-glass of cloves (whole), one-quarter of a wine-glass of allspice (whole), half a teaspoonful of mustard, quarter of a teaspoonful of ginger, quarter of a teaspoonful of cayenne, two onions (to be taken out after boiling), two-thirds of a tumblerful of vinegar; one wine-glassful of brandy to be put in after boiling. Cover and boil twenty minutes. MRS. WM. MAURICE.

CHOPPED PICKLES.

One peck of green tomatoes, two quarts of green peppers, half a peck of onions chopped fine, one teacup of sugar, one teacup of salt, two ounces of cloves, two ounces of allspice, one large nutmeg, one large tablespoonful of cinnamon, three tablespoonfuls of ginger, one pint of mustard seed, three quarts of vinegar; mix all together after the tomatoes are well drained, and boil until tender.

MRS. W. H. PULSIFER.

SPANISH PICKLES.

One peck of green tomatoes, one peck of cabbage, onions to suit the taste; chop them quite fine, then put them in a jar with a little salt mixed through them, and let them stand one day, then put them in a bag and wring as dry as possible, till into jars loosely, boil your vinegar with spices and pour over. They will be ready for use in a few days.

MRS. RICHARDS.

WESTERN PICKLES.

Beans, green tomatoes, cucumbers, onions sliced; put a layer of them in the kettle; then add a layer of salt and whole spices; till up the kettle with vinegar, let it boil once or twice; when cold add a tumbler one-third full of sweet oil and mustard. MRS. W. H. PULSIFER.

HIGDONS.

One peck of tomatoes, eight green peppers, eight onions, twelve large cucumbers, two tablespoons of whole cloves, two of allspice, and half a pint of white mustard seed; chop all the vegetables and put them in alternate layers in a stone jar, sprinkling each layer with salt; let them stand twenty-four hours; then drain dry and mix thoroughly with the mustard seed. Put the mixture in jars; boil the spice in cider vinegar, and when cold pour over the pickles. Cover closely and set in a cool place. MRS. J. M. KRUM.

CAULIFLOWER.

Sprinkle salt over layers of cauliflower, then cover with rainwater, let it stand over night, turn all into a kettle and let it come to a boil; drain the cauliflower in a cullender, scald the vinegar, and put in one-quarter of a pound of mustard, a few cloves, allspice, small onions and mustard seed; pour over the cauliflower, and bottle when cold.

RIPE CUCUMBER PICKLES.

Pare the cucumbers, slice them lengthwise, not very thin, take out the seeds, put in brine twenty-four hours, pour off, and pour on alum-water boiling hot, let it stand forty-eight hours, pour off; then to one gallon of vinegar add a pound of sugar, pepper and spice to taste, scald together and pour on boiling hot. MRS. J. PALMER, New Hampshire.

FOR ONE HUNDRED MARTINOES.

Soak in salt and water (a pint of salt to 100), changing the brine every other day, nine days, then put one ounce of cloves, one ounce of cassia, one ounce of allspice, one ounce of ginger, whole, into as much cold vinegar as will cover them when done; boil them all together until you have the strength of the spice, and pour it over the martinoes, having drained them well from the brine.

MRS. T. T. RICHARDS.

PICKLED ONIONS.

Boil until tender in milk, then pour vinegar over them
MRS. W. H. PULSIFER.

MANGO PICKLES.

One pound of race ginger, one pound of black mustard seed (swell the seed in vinegar), one pound of white mustard seed, one pound of horseradish scraped, one ounce of mace, one ounce of cloves, two ounces of allspice, four ounces of black pepper, two ounces of pulverized turmeric, four ounces of sweet oil; all the ingredients must be pulverized and mixed together. Take fifty mangoes, scrape and fill them with salt the night before you want to make them. The above ingredients will fill fifty mangoes.

CHUTNEY.

One peck of green tomatoes, one cup of salt, six large green peppers, six onions, six lemons, one cup of horseradish; chop each well and fine; drain off the tomatoes after chopping; four large cups of sugar, two tablespoonfuls of cloves, allspice and cinnamon each; cover the whole with three pints of vinegar, and boil ten or fifteen minutes. An extra nice pickle.
MRS. R. H. MORTON.

YELLOW PICKLES.

Take one pound of race ginger, lay it in water over night, one pound of garlic strung on a thread, a few small onions; salt the whole well and let them stand three days in a strong brine; one pint of mustard seed washed and dried in the sun, one ounce of best mustard, two ounces of turmeric; put these ingredients into a stone jar with two gallons of strong vinegar; then take your articles for pickles, pears, peaches, grapes, corn, beans and cauliflower, cut them in quarters and sizes to suit, and let them be salted for a week; take them out and set in the sun to dry; be careful to press the water out each day; wash them clean in salted water, wipe them on a dry towel, put them in the sun for an hour or two, then put them in your jar of preparations.

PLUM KETCHUP.

Nine pounds of plums, six pounds or sugar; boil plums and sugar together, stirring them until the plums crack open, then skim out as many of the stones as possible; boil slowly from two to four hours; add one quart of good vinegar, and boil half an hour, then add one teacup of ground spices, such as cloves, cinnamon and allspice. Bottle and seal boiling hot.

CHOW-CHOW PICKLE.

Slice thin two pecks of green tomatoes, half a peck of white onions, two dozen large green peppers, and four dozen cucumbers; salt them twenty-four hours, then drain in a bag all night; in the morning boil in weak vinegar and let them remain until next morning; pour that off, and in a large preserving kettle or pan put a layer of the sliced vegetables and a layer of brown sugar, turmeric, allspice, cloves, cinnamon, mace and white mustard seed; fill up with alternate layers, then cover with the best cider vinegar and boil until tender.

FRENCH PICKLE.

One peck of green tomatoes, cut in slices; take a layer of tomatoes and sprinkle salt over them and let them stand over night; in the morning pour off the liquor and squeeze quite dry; add three green peppers, six onions, one cabbage cut fine, one-quarter pound of white mustard seed, one-half pound of sugar, two ounces of cloves and allspice, two ounces of celery seed; mix all together and cover with vinegar; boil two hours; add vinegar when boiling if not enough.

L.

FRENCH PICKLE.

One peck of tomatoes, one-half peck of string beans, one-fourth peck of white onions, one-fourth pint of small red and green peppers, two heads of cabbage, four tablespoonfuls of white mustard seed, two tablespoonfuls of celery seed, two tablespoonfuls of whole cloves, two tablespoonfuls of allspice, one small box of yellow mustard, one pound of brown sugar; slice the tomatoes and lay in strong brine over night, then press them through a cullender, chop the cabbage and onions, break the beans, then mix all these well with the spices; put in a large kettle and cover with vinegar; boil it three hours; one ounce of turmeric.

Mrs. K. V.

EAST-INDIA PICKLES.

Take one peck of green tomatoes, one-half peck of sliced onions, four cauliflowers, salted twenty-four hours; drain them and mix with a handful of horseradish, one ounce of cloves, one ounce of cinnamon, one-quarter of a pound of white pepper, one-quarter of a pound of brown sugar, one-quarter of a pound of ground mustard seed; two ounces of chopped celery, fifty small cucumbers; put all in a kettle and cover with cold vinegar; boil fifteen minutes; put in a stone jar, and as soon as cold they are ready to eat.

PICOLILY.

Take one-half peck of green tomatoes, cut in slices the same way as the core runs, let them stand in salt over night, then drain off; add one large onion and three green peppers, one teaspoonful each of all kinds of spices, one cup of sugar, and vinegar enough to nearly cover; put the cloves in whole; cook till tender. The above will make three quarts.

PEPPER HASH.

Put your peppers in strong salt and water for three days, then cut them up fine; cut white cabbage and sprinkle with salt, letting it stand two or three hours, then squeeze it out, and mix the cabbage and peppers, sprinkle mustard seed over them; let your vinegar come to a boil, and pour over and tie up.

Mrs. Brock.

CHOW-CHOW PICKLE.

Half a peck of green tomatoes, two large heads of cabbage, fifteen large onions, twenty-five cucumbers, twelve green peppers, one pint of grated horseradish, half a pound of white mustard seed, one ounce of celery seed, some small white onions, half a teacup of ground pepper, half a cup of turmeric, half a cup of cinnamon; cut the onions, tomatoes, cucumbers, cabbage and peppers, and salt them down over night; in the morning drain off the brine and put them to soak in vinegar and water or thin vinegar; let them remain a day or two, then drain again, and mix the spices; boil one and a half gallons of vinegar and five pounds of brown sugar together and pour hot over the ingredients; do this three mornings; the third morning mix one pound of English mustard with half a pint of salad oil, then put away in jars. A nice rich pickle.

Mrs. R. H. Morton.

SWEET TOMATO PICKLES.

Half a peck of green tomatoes, one gallon of vinegar, two pounds of brown sugar, one-quarter of a pound of stick cinnamon; boil the vinegar and sugar fifteen minutes, slice the tomatoes and boil with the spice in the vinegar fifteen minutes longer; skim out the tomatoes and boil the syrup half an hour, and pour over the tomatoes; seal up in jars.

Mrs. H. M. Woodward.

PICKLED TOMATOES.

Eight pounds of green tomatoes, chop fine, and pour off the liquid, four pounds of sugar, two quarts of cider vinegar, eight or ten onions, two teaspoonfuls of salt, one tablespoonful of powdered cinnamon and cloves, and one nutmeg; boil two or three minutes.

Mrs. J. H. Palmer, New Hampshire.

PICKLED PEACHES.

To seven pounds of peaches, three pounds of light brown sugar and one quart of vinegar, one half ounce of whole cloves and mace.

PICKLED DAMSONS.

One peck of damsons, seven pounds of brown sugar, one quart of vinegar, one ounce of mace and whole cloves each.

SPICED TOMATOES.

Five pounds of tomatoes, two and a half pounds of sugar, one pint of vinegar, one tablespoonful of cloves, one tablespoonful of whole cinnamon; simmer one-half hour.

MRS. DUNCAN.

SPICED TOMATOES.

To a half bushel of tomatoes, one quart of vinegar, one quart of sugar; spice highly, boil until thick; will keep all winter; is very nice with meat. MRS. F. HEARSAM.

SPICED CURRANTS.

Five pounds of currants, four pounds of brown sugar, two tablespoonfuls of ground cloves, one tablespoonful of allspice, one-half tablespoonful of mace, one-half tablespoonful of cinnamon, one pint of vinegar.

SPICED PEACHES.

Peel your peaches (clingstones), make a syrup of two pounds of brown sugar to a pint of vinegar; put in your peaches and boil till tender; put them away with allspice, mace, cinnamon and cloves; tie the spices in muslin bags.

MRS. WM. SEMPLE.

PICKLED CHERRIES.

One gallon of cherries, two pounds of sugar, one quart of vinegar; boil the vinegar and sugar together and pour over the cherries three mornings in succession; one ounce of cinnamon, one tablespoonful of cloves, one tablespoonful of allspice.

MADAME SUBIT'S SWEET PICKLES.

Green muskmelons, pare and take out the inside, cut up and put into vinegar for a week, take out, throw away the vinegar, wipe and stick full of cinnamon and cloves; make a syrup, one pound of vinegar to one pound of melon, with three-quarters of a pound of sugar added to the vinegar; when the sugar is dissolved put in the melons and boil until you can stick a broom-straw through them, take out the melons and boil down the syrup almost to the consistency of jelly; put all together, adding a small bag of spices, and it will keep any length of time.

CANTALOPE PICKLES.

Cut the melons, which must not be quite ripe, into any shape you wish, sprinkle salt on them and let lie several hours; drain off the liquor, stripping the pieces with your fingers; weigh the melon and use half a pound of sugar to one pound of fruit; melt the sugar in a little water, boil the melon in the syrup until clear; don't put in many pieces at a time; lay them in a jar and cover with strong vinegar, set the syrup away; next day pour off this vinegar and throw it away, take as much more strong vinegar, put with the syrup and melon, add stick cinnamon and ginger root, boil all together a few moments, and put in jars.

Miss M. E. Tucker.

VERY FINE TOMATO KETCHUP.

Half a bushel of skinned tomatoes, add one quart of good vinegar, half a pound of fine table salt, a quarter of a pound of whole black pepper, one ounce of red pepper, a quarter of a pound of allspice, six good sized onions cut fine, one ounce of cloves, two pounds of brown sugar; boil the whole six hours, stirring all the time to keep from burning; when cool, strain and bottle; you can add brandy, wine or any liquor to taste, and a small quantity of garlic.

Mrs. Wm. Smith, Cin.

GOOSEBERRY KETCHUP.

Ten pounds of fruit just before ripe, five pounds of sugar, one quart of vinegar, two tablespoons each of ground pepper, cinnamon allspice and cloves; put the sugar in the vinegar and boil until dissolved, then add spices and scald well.

MRS. LEWIS E. KLINE.

CUCUMBER KETCHUP.

Grate three good sized cucumbers and one white onion, to which add one tablespoonful of grated horseradish, one of salt and one of ground black pepper; put the whole into one pint of vinegar, then bottle and cork tightly. It will keep well for one year only.

CHILI SAUCE.

Four dozen large tomatoes skinned, sixteen green peppers, seeds out, sixteen white onions, six tablespoons of salt, six tablespoons of brown sugar, four coffee-cups of vinegar; chop all fine; boil two hours, and just before taking off the fire add four ounces of celery seed.

SPANISH TOMATO SAUCE.

Twelve spoonfuls of sugar, three dozen ripe tomatoes, one and a half dozen red peppers, one dozen of onions, six teaspoonfuls of salt, twelve teacups of vinegar, six teaspoonfuls each of ginger, cinnamon and cloves; chop all fine and boil two hours. Very fine sauce.

MRS. POWELL.

TOMATO SAUCE.

One peck of green tomatoes sliced, one dozen onions sliced; sprinkle them with salt; let them stand until the next day, then drain them. Use the following spices: One small box of yellow mustard, one and a half ounces of ground black pepper, one ounce of whole cloves, one ounce of yellow mustard seed; put in the kettle a layer of spices and one of tomatoes and onions alternately; cover them with the best vinegar, a teaspoonful of turmeric; wet the mustard before putting in with the vinegar. Let the whole boil half an hour.

MRS. J. T. YOUNG.

DRINKS.

COFFEE.

Coffee should be roasted quickly in a pan in the oven, stirring every few minutes; when a bright brown, and still hot, beat up the white of an egg with a tablespoonful of melted butter, and stir up well with it. Grind just enough at a time for a single making.

BOILED COFFEE.

Stir the beaten white and shell of one egg with one-half pint of ground coffee and a very little cold water, and mix with a quart of boiling water in the coffee-boiler; boil pretty fast for twelve minutes; pour in one tablespoonful of cold water, and take from the fire; after settling for five minutes pour into the coffee-pot, which should previously be well scalded.

DRIP COFFEE.

More coffee should be allowed for a given quantity of water than if boiled and ground very fine; put the coffee in the uppermost compartment, pour on boiling water, slowly at first until the coffee is saturated, then more rapidly, shut down the top, and the coffee ought to be ready when it has passed through the strainers; if not strong enough, run it through again.

ARTIFICIAL CREAM.

Boil one quart of milk, take one teaspoonful of sugar, one teaspoonful of corn starch mixed with a little cold milk, one egg beaten very light; stir all into the boiled milk gradually, so as not to cook the egg in a curd; stir the whole until cold; this may be done more rapidly by setting the pan in cold water. MRS. POWELL.

TEA.

One teaspoonful of tea for each person, and one for the pot, is the general rule. Scald the teapot before putting in the tea and set it on the stove for one minute; pour on enough boiling water to cover it well, and let it simmer ten minutes in a warm place, but do not let it boil; put in as much boiling water as needed, and pour into a heated pot for the table.

CHOCOLATE.

Into a pint of boiling milk and water throw two divisions (two ounces) of chocolate previously cut fine, then boil it from five to seven minutes, stirring frequently.

FRENCH CHOCOLATE.

Allow two sticks of chocolate to one pint of milk; scrape the chocolate and boil it in three tablespoonfuls of milk; when the milk is boiling stir in the chocolate, after adding the whites of two eggs well whipped. Let it boil five minutes, and serve immediately. Put a tablespoonful of whipped cream in each cup before serving.

CHERRY WINE.

Two quarts of cherries, one of alcohol, three quarts of water, sugar to taste; dissolve the sugar in water, split and leave the seed in the cherries.   MRS. LEWIS E. KLINE.

MILK PUNCH.

One tumbler of milk well sweetened, two tablespoonfuls of best brandy well stirred in; suitable for invalids and given with ice.   MRS. TEASDALE.

MILK PUNCH No. 2.

Two tablespoons of old Jamaica rum, two tablespoons of sugar, or to taste, a little grated nutmeg; pour over these one pint of milk and water scalded together, half and half, or, if much fever more water than milk, if none, there may be two-thirds milk. A pint made in the morning and one in the afternoon is not too much if disposed to use it so freely.

BLACKBERRY CORDIAL.

To four gallons of berries put one gallon of water, boil about half an hour, strain through flannel or cotton; to each gallon of juice put four and a half pounds of sugar; when cool add two and a half quarts of white rum or two quarts of the best brandy, or any liquor you may prefer; put a few cloves in each bottle. Two gallons of berries and two quarts of water make one gallon of juice.

Mrs. T. T. Richards.

SPICED BLACKBERRY CORDIAL.

Take one gallon of blackberry juice, add four pounds of white sugar, boil and skim off, then add one ounce of ground cloves, one ounce of ground cinnamon, ten grated nutmegs; boil down until quite thick, then let it cool and settle; afterwards drain off and add one pint of good brandy.

Mrs. Maurice.

CREAM BEER.

Take two and a half ounces of tartaric acid, one ounce of cream tartar, two quarts of water, two pounds of sugar (brown will answer), the whites of two eggs well beaten and mixed with two tablespoonfuls of flour; put all the above articles together in a tin or brass kettle and let them scald, not boil; when cool add twenty drops of oil of lemon, or wintergreen, or whatever you like, to flavor it; bottle it and keep it in a cool place. Directions for use: Take two tablespoonfuls of the above syrup to a tumbler of water, and a half teaspoonful of soda; drink immediately.

CREAM BEER.

Two pounds of sugar, three pints of water, two ounces of tartaric acid and juice of half a lemon; scald these; when nearly cold add the beaten whites of three eggs and one-half a teacup of flour; flavor with half an ounce of wintergreen; strain and bottle and place in a cool place. Put about two tablespoons of the syrup in a glass of water; add a little soda.

RASPBERRY VINEGAR.

Put two quarts of raspberries in a large bowl, pour over them two quarts of vinegar, the next day strain the liquor on two quarts of fresh berries, let them stand a day and strain it; to each pint of liquor put one pound of white sugar, and stir until it is dissolved, put in a kettle and boil it half an hour, skim it and bottle it when cold. Blackberries are done the same way. MRS. BROCK.

CURRANT WINE.

One quart of currant juice, three quarts of water, two and a half pounds of sugar; mix well together; pour into a stone jug; let it stand until it is done working, say three weeks; bottle for use. MRS. D. R. POWELL.

CURRANT WINE.

To one quart of juice, add one quart water and four pounds of sugar. MRS. S. C. DAVIS.

CURRANT WINE.

Take currants fully ripe; mash them and strain through a jelly bag; for every quart of juice add three pounds of brown sugar and water enough to make a gallon; let it stand over night uncovered; skim and fill a clean keg, one that has held spirits is best, reserving enough to fill up as it ferments; when fermentation has ceased put the bung in tightly and keep the keg in a cool, dark place. It will be ready for use in three or four months.
MRS. O. D. FILLEY.

TOMATO WINE.

Five quarts of tomato juice, two and a half quarts of water, six pounds of white sugar; pour into jugs; cork tightly and keep until March or April, then bottle; made of yellow tomatoes is much more delicate.
MRS. H. H. SAYRE.

MEAD.

To three pounds of sugar add three pints of boiling water, one pint of molasses, one-quarter of a pound of tartaric acid and one ounce of the essence of sassafras; bottle when cold. To a tumbler nearly full of water, put two tablespoons of mead and half a teaspoon of soda.

FINE LEMONADE.

Chop up one-half of either fresh or canned pineapple; cover with white sugar and leave for a few moments to extract the juice; squeeze three large lemons into the pitcher; sweeten; add all the pineapple, and fill the pitcher with ice pounded to a snow; a glass of wine improves it if liked. In summer fresh fruits may also be added, such as strawberries, raspberries, etc. MISS LARKIN.

DISHES FOR INVALIDS.

In preparing anything for invalids, see that it is perfectly clean and as tempting as possible. Put a clean white napkin on a waiter, serve up the food in small quantities, using the best china or stoneware.

BEEF TEA.

Take some nice raw beef cut into small pieces, taking out every particle of fat or stringy part, sprinkle the pieces with a little salt, put into a thick bottle, or I think a tin farina or milk-boiler the best, and then there is no danger of any breakage; cover close, and set that into the outside boiler containing cold water; as the water gradually heats it draws the juices of the beef out better; cook about three hours, turn out into a bowl, and skim off every particle of grease, of which there should be but very little, if any; or, if there is time, let it get cold, and it can be more easily skimmed; some prefer it cold. From three to four pounds of beef makes about one pint of beef tea.

E. F. RICHARDS.

BEEF TEA No. 2.

To each pound of fresh beef (the round is the best) add one pint of cold water; cut the beef in small pieces; pour the water upon it and let it stand two hours to extract the juice; set it on the back of the stove and heat gradually to boiling point; do not let it boil; add salt to taste; a little pepper for those who like it; strain.

MUTTON BROTH.

Take a nice mutton bone with a good bit of meat attached, cover with cold water and let it cook until the meat falls from the bone in rags, strain the liquor and let it get cold, so that the fat can be easily skimmed off; season with salt, add some rice or barley, which has been previously swelled or cooked in water, to thicken: serve hot. Veal broth may be made in the same way, also chicken broth: some add a little milk.

CHICKEN JELLY.

Have the chicken well cleaned, cut up into small pieces, and crack the joints and bones well; cover with about two quarts of water, put on the back of the stove, and let it stew gently; when cooked down about half, strain the liquor off, season with salt and pepper, and skim when cool.

TOAST.

Toast water is made by breaking up some pieces of toast into a bowl, pouring over them boiling hot water: when cold strain off; add a little sugar.

Milk toast is made by pouring some hot milk seasoned with salt and thickened with a little corn starch, previously rubbed smooth with a little cold milk, over some slices of toast that have been already softened by the hot water.

A large teaspoonful of currant or cranberry jelly or barberry preserves stirred into a goblet of ice-water makes a very palatable drink for invalids.

BUTTERMILK WHEY.

Boil together one pint of sweet milk and one pint of fresh buttermilk; when the curd begins to form, strain off the liquor or whey into a pitcher, and you will have all of the most nourishing parts of both milk and buttermilk. Wine whey is made by putting a glass of wine into a pint of scalding milk; after the curd is formed, strain off the whey and sweeten.

An egg beaten, yolk and white separately, very light, put into a goblet, sweetened to taste, adding about two teaspoonfuls of any liquor, is very nourishing; or fresh sweet milk or cream can be added to the egg.

WAFERS.

Mix dry flour to a stiff dough with either milk or water; add salt and roll out as thin as possible; cut into round cakes and bake very quickly.

BLANC MANGE FOR INVALIDS.

One quart of milk, one ounce of isinglass, peel of one lemon, yolks of six eggs, one-quarter of a pound of sugar; dissolve in a quart of warm milk an ounce of fine isinglass and strain it through double muslin, put it into a clean stew-pan with the sugar and the peel of a lemon cut very thin, let it warm gently until the flavor is well extracted from the lemon, then stir it very gradually to the yolks of the eggs; return it to the stew-pan, set it on the stove until it thickens, stirring it all the time; pour it into a bowl, stir it until nearly cold, then pour it into a mould. Time, fifteen minutes.

CHICKEN CREAM.

One chicken, a pint and a half of water, three or four spoonfuls of cream; mince, then pound in a mortar the breast of a cold roast chicken, stew the remainder, with all the bones broken, in a pint and a half of water till reduced to half a pint, rub the breast through a sieve into the half pint of gravy strained off, mix them together till of the consistency of cream; when taken add three or four spoonfuls of cream and warm it in a mug in a saucepan of boiling water. Two or three spoonfuls may be taken by an invalid who cannot take animal food. Time, three-quarters of an hour.

WINE SOUP.

Beat up an egg well, both yolk and white together, boil a coffee-cup of white wine with one-half of a nutmeg and a little powdered cinnamon, stir the well-beaten egg into the wine while boiling, and add a pint of boiling milk to the wine and egg, to be constantly stirred in until well mixed; add a small quantity of white sugar if desired.

The white of one egg beaten up in ice-water and sweetened a little, is very palatable and nourishing to the sick.

MILK PORRIDGE.

One pint of milk set over the fire, one tablespoonful of sifted flour, wet smooth with a little cold milk or water; when the milk is hot stir in gradually the flour; let it boil five minutes; add salt to taste; strain before serving.

GRUEL.

Gruel can be made of either corn meal, arrowroot or oatmeal. Take about one tablespoonful of either, mix smooth with a little cold water, then pour over it one pint of boiling water, let it cook on the stove for thirty minutes, stirring frequently, add a little salt, if it thickens too much add more boiling water; some like a little sugar added, and some a little nutmeg or a little milk or cream.

INDEX.

	Page.
INTRODUCTORY	3
LIST OF CONTRIBUTORS	4
PREFACE	5
TABLE OF MEASURES	8
A WORD ABOUT COOKING	9

SOUPS.

General Directions	13	Black, or Turtle Bean	19
Pea	14	Tomato	19
Brown	14	"	20
Chicken Gumbo	14	Philadelphia Pepper Pot	20
Veal	15	Potato	20
Black Bean	15	Lobster	20
Beef	15	Beef Bouilli	21
Bean	16	Calf's Head	21
Sour Dock	16	Green Pea Pod	21
Mock Turtle	16	Mutton Broth	22
" "	17	Soup a la Reine	22
Gumbo	18	Corn Soup	22
Mock Oyster	18	Corn Chowder	22
Pilaf—Turkish Dish	19	Dumplings	23
Turtle	19	Noodles	23

FISH.

To Boil Fish	24	Lobster Farsee	26
Fried Fish	24	Fish Pudding	26
Baked Fish	24	Fish Sauce	26
Fish	25	Fresh Fish Warmed Over	26
Stewed Fish	25	Cod Fish	27
Cusk a la Creme	25	Cod Fish Relish	27
Turbot a la Creme	25	Cod Fish Balls	27
Scalloped Lobster	26	Fish Balls	27

OYSTERS.

Raw Oysters	28	Scalloped Oysters	30
Fried Oysters	28	Oysters on Toast	30
" "	29	Oyster Soup	30
Fricasseed Oysters	29	" "	31
Stewed Oysters	29	Oyster Pie	31
" "	30	Pickle Oysters	31
Scalloped Oysters	29	Oyster and Sweet Bread Pie	50

MEATS.

Boiled Meats	33
Roast Beef	33
Beef Steak	33
Yorkshire Pudding	34
Fillet of Veal	34
Roast Veal	34
Force Meat Balls	35
To Boil a Leg of Veal	35
Veal Cutlet	35
Haunch of Venison	35
Venison Steaks	36
To Corn Beef	36
Boiled Corn Beef	36
Boiled Smoked Tongue	36
Boiled Mutton	37
Cold Saddle of Mutton	37
Boiled Lamb	38
Roast Lamb	38
Roast Loin of Pork	38
Spare Rib of Pork Roasted	38
Sausage	38
Sausage Meat	39
Boiled Ham	39
Baked Ham	39
To Broil Ham	39
Potted Beef	40
Beef a la Mode	40
Spiced Beef	40
Hash	41
Meat Pie	41
To warm Cold Meats	41
Mystery	41
Beef Omelet	41
Fried Beef Steak or Lamb Chops	42
Beef Steak Smothered in Onions	42
Beef Pie	42
Frizzled Beef	42
Mock Duck	42
Savory Beef	43
Broiled Mutton Chops	43
Irish Stew	43
Liver Daub	44
Calf Liver	44
Calf's Head	44
Sausage Meat	45
To Dress Beef Kidney	45
Fried Kidney	45
Stewed Kidney	45
Tripe	46
Tripe and Oysters	46
To Fry Tripe	46
Ham Sandwiches	47
English Beef and Potato Sandwich	47
How to Cook a Leg of Mutton	47
Veal Omelet	47
" "	48
Beef Loaf	48
Welton Veal	48
Veal Loaf	48
Richamella	49
Veal Fricandeau	49
Veal Olives	49
Stew Pie of Veal	50
Sweet Breads	50
" "	52
Stewed Sweet Breads	50
A Pie of Sweet Bread and Oysters	50
Welsh Rarebit	51
Economical Croquettes	51
Sweet Bread Croquettes	52
Ham Toast	52
To use up bits of Ham	53
Pigs' Feet and Ears Soused	53
Pigs' Feet	53

GRAVIES AND SAUCES.

Drawn Butter	54
Nice for Gravy or Soup	54
Wine Sauce for Mutton or Venison	55
Oyster Sauce	55
Celery Sauce for Boiled Fowls	55
Mint Sauce for Roast Lamb	55
Venison Gravy	55

POULTRY.

Roast Turkey	56
Boiled Turkey	57
Roast Goose	57
Roast Pheasants, Partridges, etc	58
Roast Duck	58
Boiled Duck	58
Chickens	59
Chicken Pie	59

INDEX.

Quail Pie	59
Stewed Chicken with Oysters	60
Fried Chicken	60
Fricasseed Chicken	60
To Cook an Old Chicken	61
Chicken Stuffed with Oysters	61
Smothered Chicken	61
Jellied Chicken	62
Boned Chicken	62
Snipe and Woodcocks	62
Stuffed Quails	63
Small Birds Broiled	63
Potted Pigeons	63
Veal or Poultry Cake	64
Chicken Cheese	64
Chicken Saute a la Mauge	64
Chicken or Veal Croquettes	65
Chicken Croquettes	65
" "	66
Croquette of Fowl	65
Croquettes	65
"	66

SALADS.

For Chicken or Lobster	67
Salad Dressing	67
" "	68
Chicken Salad	67
Dressing for Chicken Salad	68
Potato Salad	68
Mr. T's Lettuce Dressing	69
Lettuce Salad	69
Slaw Dressing	69
Slaw Dressing	70
Cold Slaw	70
Holland Herring Salad	70
Curry Powder	70
To Mix Mustard	70
Horseradish Sauce	71
Sauce Hollandaise a la Maison Doree	71
Sauce Blanche	71

VEGETABLES.

Steam Potatoes	72
To Boil New Potatoes	72
Mashed Potatoes	72
Fried Potatoes	72
Saratoga Potatoes	73
To Broil Potatoes	73
Potatoes a la Creme	73
Potato Scollops	73
Potato Croquettes	74
Potato Rice	74
To Brown Potatoes Under Meat	74
Roast Sweet Potatoes	74
Boiled Sweet Potatoes	74
Fried Sweet Potatoes	74
Baked Tomatoes	75
Stuffed Baked Tomatoes	75
Fried Tomatoes	75
Stewed Tomatoes	75
Boiled Green Corn	75
Succotash	76
Stewed Green Corn	76
Corn Cakes, or Mock Oysters	76
Lima Beans	76
Macaroni	77
Italian Macaroni	77
Macaroni a la Creme	77
Boiled Hominy	77
Fried Hominy	77
Hominy Croquettes	78
Baked Hominy	78
Mashed Carrots	78
Boiled Carrots	78
Carrots a la Flamade	78
Fried Egg Plant	78
Baked Egg Plant	79
Egg Plant	79
To Boil Rice	79
Stewed Onions	79
Baked Spanish Onions	80
Celery	80
Celery a la Creme	80
Boiled Spinach	80
Spinach a la Creme	80
Salsify or Vegetable Oyster	81
Fried Salsify or Mock Oysters	81
Boiled Parsnips	81
Fried Parsnips	81
Parsnips, Boiled and Browned	82
Parsnips Mashed	82
Stewed Parsnips	82
Boiled Cabbage	82
Cabbage with Force Meat a la Francaise	82
Summer Squash	83
Baked Squash	83
Boiled Turnip	83
Turnips in White Sauce	83
Boiled Beets	84

Asparagus	84	Baked Beans	85
Asparagus in French Rolls	84	To Cook String Beans	86
Asparagus Pudding	84	Connecticut Baked Beans	86
Boiled Cauliflower	85	Boiled Green Peas	86
Scalloped Cauliflower	85	Stewed Green Peas	87
Caulifl'r with Parmesan Cheese	85	Green Peas a la Francaise	87

EGGS.

To keep Eggs throughout the winter	88	Egg Omelet	90
		A Nice Omelet for Breakfast	89
To Preserve Eggs	88	Omelet	90
To Boil Eggs	88	Bread Omelet	90
Poached Eggs	88	Scrambled Eggs	90
Baked Eggs	89	Egg Gems	91
Fried Eggs	89	Mumbled Eggs	91
Egg Omelet	89	Eggs on Toast	91

BREAD AND BISCUITS.

Potato Yeast	92	Beat Biscuit	100
Yeast	92	Dixie Biscuit	101
Bread	92	Milk Biscuit	101
Parker House Rolls	94	Pop-Overs	101
Light Rolls	94	Puffs or Pop-Overs	101
French Rolls	95	Tea Cake	102
Egg Biscuit	95	Soft Cake	102
French Biscuits	95	Short Cake	102
Coffee Bread	95	Drop Cakes	102
Apple or Peach Bread	96	Kirkwood Puffs	102
Corn Bread	96	Indian Cup Cake	103
Brown Bread	96	Corn Cakes	103
Graham Bread	96	Wheat Gems	103
Boston Brown Bread	97	Spanish Buns	103
" " "	107	Center Harbor Cakes	103
" " "	108	Annie's Waffles	104
Buns	97	Waffles	104
"	101	Batter Cakes	104
Rusks	97	Corn Meal Griddle Cakes	104
Mrs. R.'s Rusks	97	Buckwheat Cakes	105
Muffins	97	Squash Griddle Cakes	105
"	98	Rice Cakes	105
"	99	Corn Cakes	105
Drop Muffins	98	Stale Bread Griddle Cakes	105
Rye Muffins	98	Mock Buckwheat Cakes	105
Delicate Corn Muffins	98	Green Corn Griddle Cakes	106
Graham Flour Muffins	98	Pea Fritters	106
Sour Milk Muffins	99	Mrs. Wilson's Corn Bread	106
Sally Lun	99	Mrs. Stoddard's Corn Bread	106
Graham Rolls	99	Bannock	106
" "	100	Blueberry Cake	106
Soda Biscuit	100	Dutch Toast	107
Cream Biscuit	100	Strawberry Short Cake	107
Brighton Biscuit	100	Whortleberry Cake	107
Bolt Biscuit	100	Steamed Brown Bread	108
Cakes without Eggs	100	Boiled Bread	108

INDEX.

PUDDINGS.

Plum Pudding.................. 109	Sunderland Pudding............ 119
" " 110	Kiss Pudding.................. 119
" " 111	Corn Starch Pudding.......... 119
Steam Plum Pudding............ 109	Corn Starch Pudding Boiled... 120
Baked English Plum Pudding... 110	Planchette Pudding............ 120
Black Pudding................. 110	Chocolate Pudding............. 120
" " 121	Dandy Pudding................. 121
English Plum Pudding.......... 111	Danish Pudding................ 121
Suet Pudding.................. 111	Fritters without Milk......... 121
" " 112	Souffle Pudding............... 121
Boiled Suet Pudding........... 112	Gentleman's Pudding........... 122
President's Pudding........... 112	Eve's Pudding................. 122
Bread Pudding................. 112	Apple Meringue................ 122
Apple Bread Pudding........... 112	Jelley Meringue Pudding....... 122
Bread and Butter Pudding...... 113	Bird's Nest Pudding........... 123
Pudding Fruit................. 113	Baked Apple Dumpling Pud'ng 123
Bread Meringue................ 113	Boiled Apple Dumpling......... 123
Baked Indian Pudding.......... 113	Fruit Pudding................. 124
" " " 127	Whortleberry Pudding.......... 124
Baked Indian Pudding No. 2 ... 114	Blackberry Pudding............ 124
Boiled Indian Pudding......... 114	Citron Pudding................ 124
Corn Meal Pudding............. 114	Ginger Pudding................ 124
Rice Pudding.................. 114	Fig Pudding................... 124
Washington Pudding............ 114	Boiled Lemon Pudding.......... 125
A Delicious Rice Pudding...... 115	Lemon Pudding................. 125
Tapioca Pudding............... 115	Lemon Rice Pudding............ 125
Lemon Tapioca Pudding......... 115	Orange Pudding................ 125
Tapioca with Apples........... 116	Orange Marmalade Pudding ... 126
Huntington Pudding............ 116	Cocoanut Pudding.............. 126
Blackberry Tapioca............ 116	Old Fash'd Baked Rice Pud'ng. 126
Strawberry Tapioca............ 116	Wedding Cake Pudding.......... 126
Pineapple Tapioca............. 117	Boiled Sally Lunn Pudding..... 127
Batter Pudding................ 117	Vermicelli Pudding............ 127
Steamed Batter Pudding........ 117	Apple Fritters................ 127
Nice Batter Pudding........... 117	Corn Pudding.................. 127
Boiled Flour Pudding.......... 117	Carrot Pudding................ 128
Feather Cake Pudding.......... 118	Pudding Sauce................. 128
Cottage Pudding............... 118	Sauce......................... 128
Puff Pudding.................. 118	" 129
German Puff's................. 118	Splendid Pudding Sauce........ 128
Sponge Pudding................ 118	Aunt Mary's Sauce............. 128
" " 119	Hard Pudding Sauce............ 129

PIES.

Extra Nice.................... 130	Cocoanut Pie.................. 132
Pastry........................ 130	Raisin Pies................... 132
Chop Pastry................... 131	Mush Pies..................... 132
Mince Meat.................... 131	Transparent Pies.............. 132
Mince Pies.................... 131	Custard Pie................... 132
Summer Mince Pies............. 131	Cream Pie..................... 132
Cocoanut Pie.................. 131	Very Fine Cream Pie........... 133

INDEX.

Lemon Pies............................... 133	Apple Custard Pie.................. 136
" " 134	Apple Slump........................... 136
Splendid Lemon Pies............ 133	Apple Dowdy 137
Lemon Cheese Cakes............. 134	Connecticut Apple Pie............ 137
Golden Pie.............................. 134	Apple Pie................................ 137
Orange Pie.............................. 134	Spiced Apple Tarts.................. 137
Peach Pie................................ 135	Mock Pumpkin Pie.................. 137
Peach Cobbler......................... 135	Pumpkin Pie........................... 138
Cranberry Tart........................ 135	Cherry Pie.............................. 138
Celebrated Rhubarb Pie......... 135	Green Gooseberry Tart............ 138
Rhubarb Tart.......................... 135	Currant and Raspberry Tart..... 138
Sweet Potato Pie..................... 136	

NICE DESSERTS.

Lemon Butter......................... 139	Charlotte Russe....................... 144
Hedge-hog.............................. 139	To Make Whips...................... 145
Snow Pudding........................ 139	Lemon Creams....................... 145
Cream Snow........................... 139	Almond Custards.................... 145
Italian Snow........................... 140	English Cream........................ 145
Apple Snow............................ 140	Velvet Cream.......................... 145
Apple Float............................ 140	" " 146
Orange Souffle....................... 140	Italian Cream......................... 146
Omelet Souffle....................... 140	Spanish Cream....................... 146
" " 141	" " 149
Snow Pudding........................ 141	Isabella Cream....................... 147
Boiled Custard....................... 141	Orange Cream........................ 147
Coffee Custard....................... 141	Tapioca Cream....................... 147
Tapioca Custard..................... 141	Chocolate Gelatine.................. 147
Almond Custard..................... 142	Rice Cream............................. 148
Cream Chantilly..................... 142	Flummery............................... 149
Fine Blanc Mange.................. 142	Apples with Rice.................... 149
Spanish Blanc Mange............ 143	Orange Pudding..................... 150
Chocolate Blanc Mange......... 143	Omelet Souffle........................ 150
Ambrosia................................ 143	Caramel Custard.................... 150
Ice Apples.............................. 144	Friar's Omelet........................ 150

CONFECTIONERY.

Candy..................................... 151	Taffy Candy............................ 152
Pralines.................................. 151	Chocolate Caramels................ 152
Sugar Candy.......................... 151	Peppermints........................... 153
" " 152	Ice Cream Candy................... 153
Cream Candy......................... 151	Cream Chocolates.................. 153
White Cream Candy.............. 151	Miss Fletcher's Candy............ 153
Caramels................................ 152	French Kisses........................ 153

CAKES.

White Sponge or Angels' Food... 154	Martha Washington Tea Cake,... 156
Silver Cake............................. 155	Portsmouth Black Cake.......... 156
" " 161	Fruit Cake.............................. 156
Spread Mountain Cake.......... 155	Black Cake............................. 156
Ribbon Cake.......................... 155	Sponge Cake.......................... 157

INDEX. 241

Bread Cake	157
Sponge Cake	158
Connecticut Loaf Cake	158
White Fruit Cake	158
Chocolate Cake	158
" "	159
White Cake	159
" "	165
Velvet Cake	159
Almond Cake	159
Apple Cake	160
Spiced Marble Cake	160
Marble Cake	160
" "	161
Chocolate Marble Cake	161
Gold Cake	162
Dover Cake	162
Delicate Cake	162
Plain Fruit Cake	162
Chocolate Cream Cake	162
Lady Cake	163
Molasses Plum Cake	163
Hickory Nut Cake	163
Railroad Cake	163
Lunch Cake	163
Brides' Cake	163
Corn Starch Cake	164
Water Pound Cake	164
Eggless Cake	164
Ten Egg Cake	164
Cream Cake	164
Queen Cake	164
Fanny Cake	164
Cup Cake	165
Cider Spice Cake	165
Spice Cake	165
Munson Cake	165
Shrewsbury Cake	166
Warren Cake	166
Coffee Cake	166
Lincoln Cake	166
Cocoanut Cake	166
Almond Cake	167
Soda Cake	167
Harrison Cake	167
Date Cake	167
Feather Cake	167
Lemon Cake	167
New York Ginger Bread	168
Carrie's Ginger Bread	168
Ginger Bread	168
Soft Ginger Cake	168
Crisp Ginger Bread	168
Ginger Crisps	169
Ginger Snaps	169

LAYER CAKES.

Dame Durden Cake	170
Jelly Roll	170
Morentin Cake	170
Orange Cake	171
Lemon Cake	171
Gateau Citron	171
Poverty Cake	171
Cream for Cake Filling	172
Washington Pie	172
The Queen of Cream Pies	172
Cream	172
Roll Cake	173
White Mountain Cake	173
Mountain Cake	173
Chocolate Cake	173
Cream Cakes	174
Boston Cream Cakes	174
Lemon or Chocolate Cake	174
Mrs. Gardiner's White Cake	175
Doughnuts	175
"	176
Raised Doughnuts	175
Yankee Doughnuts	176
Crullers	176
Mrs. Clark's Crullers	177
Jumbles	177
Cookies	177
Nice Cookies without Eggs	177
Vanilla Wafers	177
Mrs. Robinson's Cookies	178
Lemon Cookies	178
Scotch Cakes	178
Cocoanut Gems	178
Macaroons	178
Wafers	179
Sugar Cakes	179
Cocoanut Jumbles	179
Sugar Ginger Snaps	179
Molasses Cookies	179
My Ginger Snaps	179
Ginger Drops	180
Molasses Drop Cake	180
Hunting Nuts	180
Crispys	180
Icing	180
"	181
Boiled Icing	180
Chocolate Cake Icing	181
Cake with Cocoanut Icing	181

16

ICE CREAM. ETC.

Ice Cream	182	Walnut Ice Cream	183
French Ice Cream	182	Biscuit Glace	183
Italian Cream	182	Frozen Pudding	183
Strawberry Ice Cream	183	Frozen Peaches	183

PRESERVES AND CANNED FRUITS.

Preserved Quinces	184	Peach Marmalade	189
Preserved Cherries	185	Peach Butter	189
Green Gage Plums	185	Grape Butter	190
Preserved Pears	185	Pineapple Brandy	190
Citron Melon Preserves	186	Brandy Peaches	190
Stewed Cranberries	186	Gelatine Jelly	190
Preserved Peaches	186	Wine Jelly	190
Grape Preserves	186	Coffee Jelly	191
Preserved Plums	187	Chocolate Mange	191
Preserved Apples for Tea	187	Strawberry, Raspberry, Blackberry Jelly	191
Good Apple Sauce	187		
Crab Apple Preserve	187	Cider Jelly	191
Blackberry Jam	187	Cranberry, Grape, Currant Jelly	192
Preserved Oranges	188	Apple Jelly	192
To Preserve Strawberries	188	To can Tomatoes Whole	192
Preserved Currants	188	Wine Jelly	192
Combination Jam	188	Canning Corn and Tomatoes	193
Conserves	188	Canned Grapes	193
Hodge Podge	189	Canned Peaches	194
Baked Pears	189	Canned Ochre and Tomatoes	194

PICKLES.

Cucumber Pickles	195	French Pickle	200
Pickled Cucumbers	196	East-India Pickles	201
Tomato Ketchup	196	Picolily	201
" "	204	Pepper Hash	201
Mixed Pickles	196	Sweet Tomato Pickles	202
Chopped Pickles	197	Pickled Tomatoes	202
Spanish Pickles	197	Pickled Peaches	202
Western Pickles	197	Pickled Damsons	203
Higdous	198	Spiced Tomatoes	203
Cauliflower	198	Spiced Currants	203
Ripe Cucumber Pickles	198	Spiced Peaches	203
For One Hundred Martinoes	198	Pickled Cherries	203
Pickled Onions	199	Madame Subit's Sweet Pickles	203
Mango Pickles	199	Cantalope Pickles	204
Chutney	199	Gooseberry Ketchup	204
Yellow Pickles	199	Cucumber Ketchup	205
Plum Ketchup	200	Chili Sauce	205
Chow Chow Pickle	200	Spanish Tomato Sauce	205
" "	201	Tomato Sauce	205

INDEX.

DRINKS.

Coffee 206	Blackberry Cordial 208
Boiled Coffee 206	Spiced Blackberry Cordial 208
Drip Coffee 206	Cream Beer 208
Artificial Cream 206	Raspberry Vinegar 209
Tea 207	Currant Wine 209
Chocolate 207	Tomato Wine 209
French Chocolate 207	Mead 210
Cherry Wine 207	Lemonade 210
Milk Punch 207	

DISHES FOR INVALIDS.

Beef Tea 211	Blanc Mange 213
Mutton Broth 211	Chicken Cream 213
Chicken Jelly 212	Wine Soup 213
Toast 212	Milk Porridge 214
Buttermilk Whey 212	Gruel 214
Wafers 213	

MEDICAL.

Management of the Sick Room 215	Hip Disease Cure 220
Diet 215	For Swollen Limbs 220
Quiet 215	Cough 220
Ventilation 215	Croup 221
Temperature 216	Baby's Sore Mouth 221
Disinfectants 216	Baby's Sour Stomach 221
Light 216	Tooth Powder 221
For Sour Stomach and to Settle Stomach After Vomiting 217	Tooth Wash 222
Convulsions 217	Chapped Hands 222
Cholera 217	Cologne 222
Apoplexy 218	Poultice 222
Epileptic Fits 218	Mustard Plaster 222
" " 218	 223
Poison Vine Eruption 218	Remedy for Burns 223
Wounds 218	Ointment for Gathered Breast ... 224
Pains in any part of the body 219	Camphor Ice 224
Rheumatism 219	Cold Cream 224
Earache 219	Bay Rum 224
For Cuts 219	Spitting Blood 224
To Relieve Dyspepsia 219	Chilblains 224
Sprains of the Wrist and Ankle. 219	Felon 225
Emetic 219	Sick Headache 225
Night Sweats 220	For Bruises 225
Weak Eyes 220	Toothache 225
For Chills and Fever 220	Nausea and Dysentery 226

MISCELLANEOUS RECEIPTS.

To Clean Marble 227	Furniture Polish 227
To Polish Clocks 227	Ants 227

INDEX.

Corns	227	Cement	230
Pretty Plants for In-Doors	228	Transparent Cement	230
Much in Little—A Useful Drug	228	Soft Soap	230
Sweetening Stone Jars	229	To Keep Calico from Fading	231
To Remove Blood Stains	229	Receipt for Washing	231
To Bake Batter Cakes	229	To Wash Silks	231
Rancid Butter	229	Cleaning Coat Collars	231
To Paint a Floor	230	To Wash Woolens	232
To Take Out Ink	230	Soap	232
To Remove Mildew and Cleanse Carpets	230	For Washing Flannel	232
		To Clean Black Crape	232

St. Louis.
Hugh R. Hildreth Printing Co.
407 Fourth Street.

COMPLETE CATALOGUE
BARR'S HOUSE FURNISHING DEPARTMENT.

KITCHEN UTENSILS.

"The New Potato Fryer,"
Refrigerators,
Ice Chests,
Water Filters,
Kitchen Tables,
Torn-down Tables,
Market Baskets,
Spring Balances,
Stamped Dish Pans,
Partition Dish Pans,
Milk Pans,
Round Cake Pans,
Octagon Cake Pans,
Fancy Cake Pans,
Jelly Cake Pans,
Sponge Cake Pans,
Lady Finger Pans,
Charlotte Russe Pans,
Croquet Moulds,
Biscuit Pans,
Gem Pans,
Puff Pans,
Corn Bread Pans,
French Roll Pans,
Bread Pans,
Muffin Pans,
Pudding Pans,
Pot Pie Pans,
Conkey Pans,
Oval Scolloped Patty Pans,
Round Scolloped Patty Pans,
Copper Saucepans,
Stove Saucepans,
Milk Boilers,
Rice Boilers,
Pudding Boilers,
Custard Boilers,
Farina Boilers,
Ham Boilers,
Vegetable Boilers,
Fish Boilers,
Soup Boilers,
Range Boilers,
Egg Boilers,
Egg Coddlers,
Coffee Boilers,
Corn Poppers,
Tea Kettles,
Tea Steepers,
Tea Pots,
Preserving Pans,
Preserving Spoons,
Preserving Skimmers,
Steak and Chop Broilers,
Game Broilers,
Oyster Broilers,
The New Stone Griddle,
Iron Griddles,
Milk Buckets,
Milk Cans,
Milk Strainers,
Milk Skimmers,
Gravy Strainers,
Basting Spoons,
Flesh Forks,
Cake Turners,
Skimmers,
Ladles,
Dippers,
Cullenders,
Egg Beaters,
Egg Timers,
Slaw Cutters,
Vegetable Slicers,
Pastry Jiggers,
Pastry Knives,
Larding Needles,
A la mode Needles,
Wooden Ladles,
Wooden Spoons,
Potato Mashers,
Cake Boxes,
Bread Boxes,
Salt Boxes,
Willow Knife Baskets,
Wooden Knife Trays,
Japanned Fork and Spoon Boxes,
Knife Cleaners,
Knife Board and Bricks,
Japanned Dredge Boxes,
Block Tin Dredge Boxes,
Japanned Pepper Boxes,
Block Tin Pepper Boxes,
Nutmeg Graters,
Bread Graters,
Epicure Broilers,
Ice Tongs,
Alaska Powder for Cleaning Paint,
French Vegetable Cutters,
English Vegetable Knives,
Plain Patty Pans,
Taffy Pans,
Omelette Pans,
Fish Pans,
Fry Pans,
Dripping Pans,
Pie Plates,
Pastry or Pie Boards,
Biscuit Beaters,
Rolling Pins,
Biscuit Cutters,
Cake Cutters,
Pastry Form Cutters,
Cream Whips,
Egg Whips,
Revolving Egg Beaters,
Ice Cream Freezers,
Ice Cream Spoons,
Ice Picks,
Jelly Moulds,
Pudding Moulds,
Butter Moulds,
Butter Ladles,
Butter Buckets,
Apple Parers,
Peach Parers,
Potato Parers,
Cherry Stoners,
Apple Corers,
Lemon Squeezers,
Porcelain-lined Saucepans,
Tin-lined Saucepans,
Jelly Strainers,
Tea Strainers,
Bread Bowls,
Flour Sieves,
Flour Seive and Scoop Combined,
Flour and Sugar Scoops,
Flour Buckets,
Flour Barrel Covers,
Sugar Sieves,
Sugar Boxes,
Sugar Buckets,
Coffee Roasters,
Coffee Mills,
Spice Mills,
Spice Boxes,
Coffee Strainers,
Plain Tin Coffee Pots,
Block Tin Coffee Pots,
Drip Coffee Pots,
National Coffee Pots,
Coffee Biggins,
Meat Cutters,
Meat Saws,
Meat Skewers,
Meat Boards,
Meat Pounders,
Meat Knives,
Butcher Knives,
Boning Knives,
Bread Knives,
Ham Saw Knives,
Chopping Knives,
Chopping Trays,
Rubber Force Cups,
Horse Radish Graters,
Tin Funnels,
Tin Measures,
Tin Buckets, all sizes,
Pint and Quart Cups,
Dish Baskets, lined with Tin,
Cup Mops,
Bottle Washers,
Cork Pullers,
Cork Screws,
Silver Plate Brushes,
Silver Polish Powder,
Silver Soap,
Waffle Irons,
Kitchen Knives and Forks,
Kitchen Table and Tea Spoons,
Stove Cover Lifters,
Kitchen Shovels and Tongs,
Kitchen Knife Stone,
Towel Rollers,
Roach Traps,
Fly Traps,
Wash Basins,
Soap Dishes,
Chain Pot Cleaners,
Ice Cream Freezers,
Churns,
Patent Roasting Pan,
Magic Flour Sifters,
International Coffee Pot,
Vienna Coffee Machine,
Oil Stoves.

ARTICLES FOR DINING-ROOM.

Ivory Handle Table and Dessert Knives,
Ivory Handle Carvers and Steels,
Rubber Handle Table and Dessert Knives,
Rubber Handle Carvers and Steels,
Knives & Forks of all Kinds,
Game Carvers and Forks,
Knife and Fork Rests,
Knife Washers,
Knife Sharpeners,
Silver-plated Table Forks,
Silver-plated Dessert Forks,
Silver-plated Table Spoons,
Silver-plated Dessert Spoons,
Silver-plated Tea Spoons,
Silver-plated Sugar Spoons,
Silver-plated Soup Ladles,
Silver-plated Oyster Ladles,
Silver-plated Gravy Ladles,
Silver-plated Cream Ladles,
Silver-plated Butter Knives,
Silver-plated Nutcracks,
Silver-plated Nutpicks,
Silver-plated Tea Sets,
Silver-plated Breakfast Casters,
Britannia Tea Sets,
Britannia Coffee Pots,
Britannia Tea Pots,
Britannia Sugar Bowls,
Britannia Cream Pitchers,
Britannia Water Pitchers,
Block Tin Chafing Dishes,
Block Tin Coffee and Tea Urns,
Block Tin Soup Tureens,
Block Tin Tea and Coffee Pots,
Crumb Brushes and Trays,
Butlers' Trays and Stands,
Waiters,
Table Mats,
Silver-plated Dinner Casters,
Silver-plated Pickle Casters,
Silver-plated Syrup Pitchers,
Silver-plated Cake Baskets,
Silver-plated Ice Pitchers,
Silver-plated Butter Dishes,
Silver-plated Salvers,
Silver-plated Hand Waiters,
Silver-plated Pressure Bells,
Silver-plated Napkin Rings,
Sherwood's Wire Coffeepot Stands,
Sherwood's Wire Cake and Fruit Baskets,
Sherwood's Wire Breakfast Casters,
Sherwood's Wire Dish Covers,
Egg Coddlers,
Knife, Fork and Spoon Baskets,
Wine Coolers,
Champagne Openers,
Corkscrews,
Tin Can Openers,
Bread Knives,
Water Coolers,
Water Pitchers,
Emery Knife Sharpeners,
Child's Table Trays,
Fly Brushes,
Fire Sets and Stands,
Hair Floor Brushes,
Tooth Picks,
Tile Coffee Pot Stands,
Chamois Skins,
Wine Coolers,
Water Filters,
Cooler Stands,
Patent Gotham Water Coolers,
Whisk Broom Holders,
Glove Boxes,
Hdkchf Boxes,
Adjustable Window Screens,
Fly Traps,
Emery Knife Sharpeners,
Tea Trays,
Bread Trays,
Britannia Casters,
Salad Spoons and Forks.

WM. BARR DRY GOODS CO.
Sixth, Olive to Locust Street, St. Louis.

SIMMONS HARDWARE CO.

Ninth Street and Washington Ave.,

CARRY A MOST COMPLETE ASSORTMENT OF

Hardware, Cutlery

AND

HOUSE FURNISHING GOODS,

ALSO

BABY CARRIAGES, BIRD CAGES, &c.

AND SELL THEM

At Such Exceedingly Low Prices

AS TO MAKE IT VERY PROFITABLE TO THE CUSTOMER.

THEIR ASSORTMENT OF

House Furnishing Goods

AND

SILVER PLATED WARE

IS THE LARGEST EVER OFFERED IN THE WEST.

WE INVITE ATTENTION TO OUR

SUPERB STOCK

OF

DIAMONDS, WATCHES, JEWELRY, SILVERWARE, PLATEDWARE, CUTLERY, MUSIC BOXES

and FINE POTTERIES,

Which we offer at Lower Prices than any Establishment East or West.

CALL, EXAMINE AND BE CONVINCED.

MERMOD, JACCARD & CO.

Corner Fourth and Locust Streets.

All Goods Marked in Plain Figures, and but One Price.

FINE SILK UMBRELLAS, CHOICE STOCK, LOW PRICES.

HUGH R. HILDRETH PRINTING CO.

Call or Send for Catalogues of

**Miscellaneous Books,
Medical Books,
Theological Books,
Catholic Literature,
Scientific and
Agricultural Books,
Holiday Gift Books,
English Books,
Juvenile Books,**

MANY OF THESE BOOKS ARE OFFERED
AT ONE-HALF THE PUBLISHERS' PRICES.

We will Mail these Catalogues to any Address when Desired.

HUGH R. HILDRETH PRINTING CO.

407 N. Fourth Street, St. Louis.

www.ingramcontent.com/pod-product-compliance
Lightning Source LLC
Chambersburg PA
CBHW021829230426
43669CB00008B/913